MW00438921

Community

HENRI J.M. NOUWEN

Community

Edited by Stephen Lazarus

ORBIS BOOKS
Maryknoll, New York 10545

Maryknoll, New York 10545

Founded in 1970, Orbis Books endeavors to publish works that enlighten the mind, nourish the spirit, and challenge the conscience. The publishing arm of the Maryknoll Fathers and Brothers, Orbis seeks to explore the global dimensions of the Christian faith and mission, to invite dialogue with diverse cultures and religious traditions, and to serve the cause of reconciliation and peace. The books published reflect the views of their authors and do not represent the official position of the Maryknoll Society. To learn more about Maryknoll and Orbis Books, please visit our website at www.orbisbooks.com.

Manufactured in the United States of America

Library of Congress Cataloging-in-Publication Data

Names: Nouwen, Henri J. M., author. | Lazarus, Stephen, editor.
Title: Community / Henri J. M. Nouwen ; edited by Stephen Lazarus.
Description: Maryknoll, NY : Orbis Books, [2021] | Includes bibliographical references. | Summary: "Essays and talks on the theme of community by Henri Nouwen, the popular writer and spiritual teacher"—Provided by publisher.
Identifiers: LCCN 2021008684 (print) | LCCN 2021008685 (ebook) | ISBN 9781626984394 (cloth) | ISBN 9781608339020 (ebook)
Subjects: LCSH: Communities—Religious aspects—Catholic Church.
Classification: LCC BV625 .N68 2021 (print) | LCC BV625 (ebook) | DDC 261/.1—dc23
LC record available at https://lccn.loc.gov/2021008684
LC ebook record available at https://lccn.loc.gov/2021008685

Contents

Foreword

The seeds of this volume actually date back more than forty years to my earliest encounters with Henri Nouwen. At the time I was the managing editor of *The Catholic Worker,* the newspaper founded by Dorothy Day. At 22, I was not a terribly experienced editor; I was not an experienced anything, for that matter. Henri, in contrast, was a distinguished professor at Yale Divinity School and a writer of growing repute, though I had not actually read any of his books. Nevertheless, I asked him if he would like to contribute something to the *Worker*, and he responded graciously, offering three essays on the subject of community. I don't know what I was expecting, but I was not terribly impressed. Frankly, they struck me as abstract and impersonal—out of character with stories in the *Worker* that were typically rooted in concrete, everyday life.

After some time had passed, Henri asked me what I thought of his pieces. Even allowing for my youth, my response was singularly lame. "Uh, thanks," I said weakly. "Do you have anything else?" From his expression I could see at once how badly I had misplayed my hand. "I just gave you *three* articles!" he said, understandably miffed.

What I meant to say, I hastened to assure him, was that I had every intention of publishing *one* of his fine essays—which I did. But he never offered us anything else, and I didn't ask again.

(Ten years later, when I told him that I had been offered the job as editor-in-chief at Orbis Books he told me that if anyone asked him, he would say that intellectually I was a perfect fit, but he didn't think I had the "human gifts" for this type of work. *Touché!*)

Though I would later recall this story, it was only recently, when invited to give a talk on the "Counter-Cultural Spirituality of Henri Nouwen," that I bothered to look back on his original essay. (It appears in this volume as chapter Four: "The Faces of Community.") When I finally did, I could see why it hadn't appealed to me. It was indeed abstract. It didn't sound like it was written by someone who had a lot of actual experience of community. But on this rereading I was struck by other, profound qualities that had gone over my twenty-two-year-old head.

In many ways Henri's essay touched on themes that would appear throughout his work. He wrote about how our culture encourages us to focus on what makes us different from other people, concerned with how to impress others and how to communicate our sense of being special. "Jesus Christ," he wrote, "reveals to us that our real identity is not to be found on the edges of our existence where we can brag about our specialties, but in the center where we can recognize our basic human sameness, and discover each other as brothers and sisters, children of the same God."

At that time I really couldn't understand what Henri was talking about; it didn't seem to speak to the practical problems of community life, as I experienced them—for instance, the fact that I didn't seem to be getting as much credit for my work on the paper as I thought I deserved! "To live the Christian life," Henri wrote, "requires a radical conversion. It requires us to look for our identity not where we are different or outstanding but where we are the same." He spoke of the need to "recognize our common human brokenness and our common need for healing." While I was very aware of the failings of everyone around me back then, I didn't have any sense of my own human brokenness or my need for healing. When I eventually did, I gave up editing *The Catholic Worker.* And Henri would play a significant role in the journey that followed.

But now, inspired by my rereading of that essay I proposed to the Nouwen Trust that we seek out and publish Henri's original three-part series on community. Strangely, the Nouwen archives yielded no trace of that series. But instead Stephen Lazarus has produced something much better: a collection of Henri's reflections on community, spanning his early pieces from the 1970s to later articles and talks, many of them drawn from his experience in the L'Arche Daybreak Community, his home for the last ten years of his life. From these pieces we can see not only the continuity in Henri's commitment to the pursuit of community, but his movement from an attitude that was arguably abstract and impersonal, to something concrete and real. That movement was true of all the writings following his arrival at Daybreak. Whether the subject was community, peacemaking, discipleship, or solidarity with the poor, he wrote about what he had seen and known firsthand. He had undergone the "radical conversion" he had described in that article of so many years ago—steadily growing into the ideas he had explored in his earlier writings.

As any serious reader of Henri's books, particularly his journals, is aware, Henri was afflicted by a deep need for affirmation and affection, and a restless search for home. He moved from Notre Dame to Yale and then to Harvard Divinity School. Along the way he tried living in a Trappist monastery and working in the missions in Latin America. As he wrote in one of his early books, he was constantly "driven from one book to another, one place to another, one project to another."

He hoped he would emerge from his time with the Trappists "a different person, more integrated, more spiritual, more virtuous, more compassionate, more gentle, and more joyful." But this was an illusion.

Many years later, *In the Road to Daybreak,* the journal of his year with the L'Arche community in France, he continued to describe his difficulties with the same old struggles with rejection, his extreme sensitivity, his propensity to fill his every moment with projects and busy-ness. A priest, to whom he shared his restlessness, told him the obvious: "The issue is not where you are, but how you live wherever you are." That had not changed by the end of his time in France. "I am still the restless, nervous, intense, distracted, and impulse-driven person I was when I set out on this spiritual journey." But that was only one side of Henri—the desire to outrun and escape the claims of his own wounded and conflictive nature. The other side, beneath all this restless searching, was his unending effort to run toward Jesus and the insight that where Jesus was to be found was not in success, glory, or the applause of the crowd; it was a path of downward mobility, toward the poor, the marginalized, and the ordinary.

Ultimately it was at the L'Arche Daybreak Community that he found the home he was seeking. There, where he was accepted and loved just for being Henri—quite apart from his achievements and his books—he found the pathway to his own healing. This was not because his own brokenness was somehow mended, but because there he finally found a place where his own brokenness could be the doorway to resurrection.

For many years, Henri had sought to find in friendship or community a solution to the gaping desire and vulnerability in his heart. But this was not, as he came to acknowledge, what community is for. At Daybreak, he finally embraced the truth

that we do not have be healed and whole before living our vocation as God's beloved sons and daughters. Of course, Henri
already knew all that; he had written books about it. But it was
only real for him when he actually lived in community, with
people unafraid to share their own vulnerability. Only in this
context could he genuinely know and accept his true belovedness.

In the journal of his final Sabbatical year, just months before
his death, he acknowledged his inner wound—his "immense
need for affection, and this immense fear of rejection." Probably, he recognized, this wound would never go away. It was
there to stay. But he had come to a deep insight—that perhaps
this wound "is a gateway to my salvation, a door to glory, and
a passage to freedom. I am aware that this wound of mine is
a gift in disguise. These many short but intense experiences of
abandonment lead me to the place where I'm learning to let go
of fear and surrender my spirit into the hands of One whose
acceptance has no limits."

The final talk in this volume is taken from that last year.
There he speaks of "the constant need of conversion that we have
in life. Conversion from a heart of stone to a heart of flesh."
He writes about many of the same themes to be found in the
essay he gave me twenty years before: about how we measure
ourselves in terms of our productivity and construct an identity around the things that differentiate us from other people.
"What an enormous, important spiritual journey it is when we
discover that where our healing begins is where joy is rooted.
Not in where you are different from people, but in where you
are the same."

The conversion he maps is from self-rejection to self-acceptance, from competition to compassion, from productivity to
fruitfulness. "That is what creates community." It was another

variation on the themes he had shared with me so many years ago. Had I finally acquired the "human gifts" to understand what Henri was saying? Or had he found a different voice—"more compassionate, more gentle, and more joyful"?

It is sad to read, in this talk from December 1995, his speculation: "I might be dead in ten years." In fact, his sudden death followed only nine months later. I remember it well. At that time I was working with Henri on his final book, *Adam: God's Beloved.* Published posthumously, it was a fitting summation of his personal "creed." And yet other books, including this one, published twenty-five years after his death, have continued to appear. As Henri learned, our lives are not measured by our productivity, but by our fruitfulness. Seeds that fell on rocky soil, more than forty years ago, have borne fruit. May this book plant future seeds.

ROBERT ELLSBERG
Publisher

Introduction

Henri Nouwen wrote and spoke often about community during his life and ministry as a pastor, priest, and a professor. His search for community propelled his writing and many of his life's most significant choices, including his decision to leave his academic teaching position at Harvard in 1986 to join a L'Arche community, Daybreak, in Richmond Hill, Ontario. It was as part of the Daybreak community that Henri lived the last ten years of his life alongside those with intellectual and developmental disabilities and their assistants. Drawing on published and previously unpublished material, this book provides a picture of why Henri thought community was such a necessary and integral part of the spiritual life in all its many dimensions.

For Henri, community is a basic need and hunger of the human heart. We are created for community, but often we do not experience it in the individualistic and competitive cultures that shape our lives. Community is a place marked by acceptance, intimacy, and vulnerability, where we can bear fruit in solidarity with others and be the body of Christ for the sake of the world. It is a place of care and celebration, the place where our wounds and weaknesses are exposed, a sheltered place for the confession of sin and brokenness, and a house of love where we can receive forgiveness and offer it in return.

Community for Henri was also a difficult and lifelong quest.

It was a quest for belonging with others and for belonging to God that in his writing and speaking he called communion. Community includes the great gifts he discovered as a beloved member of Daybreak, an intentional Christian community, and at the Abbey of the Genesee, a Trappist monastery where he made extended stays and sought spiritual guidance. It also can be found in the ordinary (and sometimes extraordinary) experiences of life together with others in friendships and in families, in worshiping congregations, and in small groups where people come together with a common purpose. For Henri, it is in community in its many different forms where we can rediscover and claim our shared humanity and our vulnerability to be empowered to live more compassionately. Encouraged by others and the example of Jesus, we can practice together what Henri called "the downward way of Christ" that does not run away from human suffering but responds with love and care. We are able to do that because we have discovered and claimed our own belovedness in God that extends outward to all without exception or condition.

Among his thirty-nine published books, translated into many languages, Henri authored eight books between 1969 and 1986 that include substantial chapters on community.[1] Most of his other books also explore dimensions of this theme implicitly or explicitly, incorporating insights about community, such as those that can be found in his well-known daily devotional *Bread for the Journey*, or his book *Can You Drink the Cup?*, both completed in 1996, the last year of his life. In *Can You Drink*

---

[1] These include *Intimacy* (1969); *Out of Solitude* (1974); *Reaching Out* (1975); *Clowning in Rome* (1979); *Making All Things New* (1981); *Compassion* (1982); *Peacework* (authored 1982–1984); and *Behold the Beauty of the Lord* (published 1987).

the Cup?, Henri writes: "Community is a fellowship of people who do not hide their joys or sorrows but make them visible to each other in a gesture of hope. . . . Community is like a large mosaic . . . a fellowship of little people who together make God visible to the world."[2]

Beyond these published books, Henri spoke frequently about community in lectures and on retreats across North America and Europe. He also contributed many short articles on the topic to various publications from the 1970s until the time of his death in 1996. He died from a sudden heart attack in his home country of the Netherlands while en route to make a film in Saint Petersburg, Russia, about his book *The Return of the Prodigal Son*. This book gathers together some of those lesser-known articles and presentations, including five appearing in print here for the first time. Looking back at his writing and speaking on community over more than two decades, this book marks the 25th anniversary of his death, and the ongoing relevance of his insights for a world in need of the kind of community he described.

The chapters are organized chronologically from the 1970s to the 1990s, with the exception of the first chapter, which is a presentation Henri delivered on solitude, community, and ministry in 1993. It is followed by an article on spiritual formation and community in theological education that Henri published in 1977 during his ten years as a professor of pastoral theology at Yale Divinity School. In that article he explores the communal context of Christian spirituality and theological education, in addition to the role of spiritual practices such as lectio divina, prayer, silence, and spiritual direction. Chapter 3 explores the

---

[2]*Can You Drink the Cup?* (Notre Dame, IN: Ave Maria Press, 1996), 57–58.

integral link between community and solitude for communities at risk of burnout, observing how time alone and apart makes community members stronger when they are together. Solitude, he explains, is also much more than simply a means to some positive end. "Without solitude," he writes, "a prophetic community loses its pastoral dimension and soon extinguishes its own light."

Chapter 4 explores how living in community requires a radical change of heart and mind for most people today. Community requires "living with the mind of Christ," Henri writes, and it "starts becoming visible as soon as we perceive ourselves as fellow travelers, as people on the same road." In chapter 5 (originally a sermon Henri gave to mark the United Nations General Assembly's Second Special Session on Disarmament in 1982) Henri discusses the role of community and prayer in peacemaking. "Community provides the space where through prayer and a careful diagnosis of the problems of our day, we feel called to speak up and act together," he preaches.

In chapter 6, Henri explores the interactions between the broken self, the broken world, and community in an address to the Catholic Youth Corps given in 1987 less than a year after he accepted the call to join the community of L'Arche Daybreak. Chapter 7 recounts the story of Henri's visit to another L'Arche community, one in Central America in the 1980s. Here he explores what communities like the one he visited in Suyapa, Honduras, have to teach Christians in North America about community, systemic injustice, and faithfulness to Jesus and the Kingdom of God. In chapter 8, as part of a previously unpublished lecture from 1991, Henri recounts how his move from the competitive academic atmosphere of Harvard to Daybreak deepened his own understanding and practice of community, though not without considerable pain and struggle, even as he found the home he had been seeking for many years. We see the consistency of his insights over time, as well as their maturing through a more lived-out experience of community.

In chapter 9, Henri offers a spirituality for community that incorporates lessons learned from his pastoring, caregiving, and care-receiving at L'Arche. Not one ever to paper over the genuine stress and struggle of community, Henri notes humorously: "Community is the place where the person you least want to live with always lives." The concluding chapter offers an extended retreat presentation Henri gave to assistants at a L'Arche community in the final year of his life. He spoke on the need for conversion and transformation in community life, offering counsel and spiritual practices to keep community life focused on the compassionate and life-giving way of Jesus.

Community, for Henri, was never first of all an abstract or academic or optional idea. Life together and the bonds of connection and belonging that we depend on daily are as immediate and necessary for life as one's next breath. That fact has become powerfully apparent as the entire world continues to deal with the disruptive and devastating impact of the global COVID-19 pandemic. The development of this book to mark the 25th anniversary of Henri's death coincided with the outbreak of a contagious and deadly disease that has closed churches and workplaces, separated children from grandparents, ended normal gatherings, and altered the experience of community that many took for granted before February 2020. Long remembered will be the imposed isolation from one another, the loneliness, the mandated lockdowns for the sake of public health, and the tragic loss of life. Into this experience of a radical absence of life together that many experience today, Henri's words and insights about community, and our human need for it, take on a great urgency that only adds to their deep and abiding wisdom.

Stephen Lazarus
The Sunday before Ash Wednesday
February 14, 2021

From Solitude to Community to Ministry

In this address Henri describes how following Jesus involves the spiritual practice of creating space for God through solitude, community, and ministry. He presented this talk at a conference in Toronto in the fall of 1993, three years before his death.

The word *discipleship* and the word *discipline* are the same word, which has always fascinated me. Once you have made the choice to say, "Yes, I want to follow Jesus," the question is, "What disciplines will help me remain faithful to that choice?" If we want to be disciples of Jesus, we have to live a disciplined life.

By discipline, I do not mean control. If I know the discipline of psychology or of economics, I have a certain control over a body of knowledge. If I discipline my children, I want to have a little control over them.

But in the spiritual life, the word *discipline* means "the effort to create some space in which God can act." Discipline means to prevent everything in your life from being filled up. Discipline means that somewhere you're not occupied, and certainly not preoccupied. In the spiritual life, discipline means to create that space in which something can happen that you hadn't planned or counted on.

I think three disciplines are important for us to remain faithful, so we not only become disciples, but also remain disciples. These disciplines are contained in one passage from scripture with which we're familiar, but one that we may be surprised to find speaks about discipline.

"Now it happened in those days that Jesus went onto the mountain to pray, and he spent the whole night in prayer to God. When day came, he summoned his disciples and picked out twelve of them and called them apostles: Simon, whom he called Peter; and his brother, Andrew; James; John; Philip; Bartholomew; Matthew; Thomas; James, son of Alphaeus; Simon, called the Zealot; Judas, son of James; and Judas Iscariot, who became a traitor.

"He then came down with them and stopped at a piece of level ground where there was a large gathering of his disciples. There was a great crowd of people from all parts of Judea and Jerusalem and the coastal region of Tyre and Sidon, who had come to hear him and be cured of their diseases. And people tormented by unclean spirits were also cured. Everyone in the crowd was trying to touch him because power came out of him that cured them all" (Luke 6:12–19).

This is a beautiful story that moves from night to morning to afternoon. Jesus spent the night in solitude with God. In the morning, he gathered his apostles around him and formed community. In the afternoon, with his apostles, he went out and preached the Word and healed the sick.

Notice the order: from solitude to community to ministry. The night is for solitude; the morning for community; the afternoon for ministry. So often in ministry, I have wanted to do it by myself. If it didn't work, I went to others and said, "Please!" searching for a community to help me. If that didn't work, maybe I'd start praying.

But the order that Jesus teaches us is the reverse. It begins by being with God in solitude; then it creates a fellowship, a community with whom the mission is being lived; and finally this community goes out together to heal and to proclaim good news.

I believe you can look at solitude, community, and ministry as three disciplines by which we create space for God. If we create space in which God can act and speak, something surprising will happen. You and I are called to these disciplines if we want to be disciples.

Solitude

Solitude is being with God and God alone. Is there any space for that in your life?

Why is it so important that you are with God and God alone on the mountaintop? It's important because it's the place in which you can listen to the voice of the One who calls you the beloved. To pray is to listen to the One who calls you "my beloved daughter," "my beloved son," "my beloved child." To pray is to let that voice speak to the center of your being, to your guts, and let that voice resound in your whole being.

Who am I? I am the beloved. That's the voice Jesus heard

when he came out of the Jordan River: "You are my beloved; on you my favor rests." And Jesus says to you and to me that we are loved as he is loved. That same voice is there for you. When you are not claiming that voice, you cannot walk freely in this world.

Jesus listened to that voice all the time, and he was able to walk right through life. People were applauding him, laughing at him; praising him and rejecting him; calling "Hosanna!" and calling "Crucify!" But in the midst of that, Jesus knew one thing—I am the beloved; I am God's favorite one. He clung to that voice.

If we create space in which God can act and speak, something surprising will happen.

There are many other voices speaking—loudly: "Prove that you are the beloved." "Prove you're worth something." "Prove you have any contribution to make." "Do something relevant." "Be sure you make a name for yourself." "At least have some power—then people will love you; then people will say you're wonderful, you're great."

These voices are so strong in this world. These were the voices Jesus heard right after he heard, "You are my beloved." Another voice said, "Prove you are the beloved. Do something. Change these stones into bread. Be sure you're famous. Jump from the temple, and you will be known. Grab some power so you have real influence. Don't you want some influence? Isn't that why you came?"

Jesus said, "No, I don't have to prove anything. I am already the beloved."

I love Rembrandt's painting "The Return of the Prodigal Son." The father holds his son, holds his daughter, and touches his son and his daughter and says, "You are my beloved. I'm not going to ask you any questions. Wherever you have gone, whatever you have done, and whatever people say about you,

you're my beloved. I hold you safe in my embrace. I touch you. I hold you safe under my wings. You can come home to me whose name is Compassionate, whose name is Love."

If you keep that in mind, you can deal with an enormous amount of success as well as an enormous amount of failure without losing your identity, because your identity is that you are the beloved. Long before your father and mother, your brothers and sisters, your teachers, your church, or any people touched you in a loving as well as in a wounding way—long before you were rejected by some person or praised by somebody else—that voice has been there always. "I have loved you with an everlasting love." That love is there before you were born and will be there after you die.

A life of 50, 60, 70, or 100 years is just a little moment in which you can say, "Yes, I love you too." God has become so vulnerable, so little, so dependent in a manger and on a cross and is begging us, "Do you love me? Do you love me? Do you really love me?"

That's where ministry starts, because your freedom is anchored in claiming your belovedness. That allows you to go into this world and touch people, heal them, speak with them, and make them aware that they are beloved, chosen, and blessed. When you discover your belovedness by God, you see the belovedness of other people and call that forth. It's an incredible mystery of God's love that the more you know how deeply you are loved, the more you will see how deeply your sisters and your brothers in the human family are loved.

Now this is not easy. Jesus spent *the night* in prayer. That's a picture of the fact that prayer is not something you always feel. It's not a voice you always hear with these ears. It's not always an insight that suddenly comes to you in your little mind. (God's heart is greater than the human heart, God's mind is greater than the human mind, and God's light is so great that it might blind you and make you feel like you're in the night.)

But you have to pray. You have to listen to the voice who calls you the beloved, because otherwise you will run around begging for affirmation, for praise, for success. And then you're not free.

Oh, if we could sit for just one half hour a day doing nothing except taking a simple word from the gospel and putting it in front of us—say, "The Lord is my shepherd; there is nothing I shall want." Say it three times, and we know it's not true, because we want many things. That's exactly why we're so nervous. But if we keep saying the truth, the real truth—"The Lord is my shepherd; there is nothing I shall want"—and let that truth descend from our mind into our heart, gradually those words are written on the walls of our inner holy place. That becomes the space in which we can receive our colleagues and our work, our family and our friends, and the people whom we will meet during the day.

The trouble is, as soon as you sit and become quiet, you think, *Oh, I forgot this. I should call my friend. Later on I'm going to see him.* Your inner life is like a banana tree filled with monkeys jumping up and down.

It's not easy to sit and trust that in solitude God will speak to you—not as a magical voice but that he will let you know something gradually over the years. And in that word from God you will find the inner place from which to live your life.

Solitude is where spiritual ministry begins. That's where Jesus listened to God. That's where we listen to God.

Sometimes I think of life as a big wagon wheel with many spokes. In the middle is the hub. Often in ministry, it looks like we are running around the rim trying to reach everybody. But God says, "Start in the hub; live in the hub. Then you will be connected with all the spokes, and you won't have to run so fast."

Community

It's precisely in the hub, in that communion with God, that we discover the call to community. It's remarkable that solitude always calls us to community. In solitude you realize you're part of a human family and that you want to live something together.

By community, I don't mean formal communities. I mean families, friends, parishes, twelve-step programs, prayer groups. Community is not an organization; community is a way of living: you gather around you people with whom you want to proclaim the truth that we are the beloved sons and daughters of God.

Community is not easy. Somebody once said, "Community is the place where the person you least want to live with always lives." In Jesus' community of twelve apostles, the last name was that of someone who was going to betray him. That person is always in your community somewhere; in the eyes of others, you might be that person.

I live in a community called Daybreak—one of over a hundred communities throughout the world where children, men, and women who are mentally disabled and those who assist them live together. We share all aspects of day-to-day living. Nathan, Janet, and all the other people of our community know how hard it is and how beautiful it is to live together.

Why is it so important that solitude come before community? If we do not know we are the beloved sons and daughters of God, we're going to expect someone in the community to make us feel that way. They cannot. We'll expect someone to give us that perfect, unconditional love. But community is not loneliness grabbing onto loneliness: "I'm so lonely, and you're so lonely." It's solitude grabbing onto solitude: "I am the beloved;

you are the beloved; together we can build a home." Sometimes you are close, and that's wonderful. Sometimes you don't feel much love, and that's hard. But we can be faithful. We can build a home together and create space for God and for the children of God.

Within the discipline of community are the disciplines of forgiveness and celebration. Forgiveness and celebration are what make community, whether a marriage, a friendship, or any other form of community.

What is forgiveness? Forgiveness is to allow the other person not to be God. Forgiveness says, "I know you love me, but you don't have to love me unconditionally, because no human being can do that."

We all have wounds. We all are in so much pain. It's precisely this feeling of loneliness that lurks behind all our successes, that feeling of uselessness that hides under all the praise, that feeling of meaninglessness even when people say we are fantastic—that is what makes us sometimes grab onto people and expect from them an affection and love they cannot give.

If we want other people to give us something that only God can give, we become a demon. We say, "Love me!" and before you know it we become violent and demanding and manipulative. It's so important that we keep forgiving one another—not once in a while, but every moment of life. Before you have had your breakfast, you have already had at least three opportunities to forgive people, because your mind is already wondering, *What will they think about me? What will he or she do? How will they use me?*

To forgive other people for being able to give you only a little love—that's a hard discipline. To keep asking others for forgiveness because you can give only a little love—that's a hard discipline, too. It hurts to say to your children, to your wife or your husband, to your friends, that you cannot give them all that you would like to give. Still, that is where community starts to be created, when we come together in a forgiving and undemanding way.

If you know you're God's beloved, you can deal with an enormous amount of success as well as an enormous amount of failure.

This is where celebration, the second discipline of community, comes in. If you can forgive that another person cannot give you what only God can give, then you can celebrate that person's gift. Then you can see the love that person is giving you as a reflection of God's great unconditional love. "Love one another because I have loved you first." When we have known that first love, we can see the love that comes to us from people as the reflection of that. We can celebrate that and say, "Wow, that's beautiful!"

In our community, Daybreak, we have to do a lot of forgiving. But right in the midst of forgiving comes a celebration: we see the beauty of people who quite often are considered marginal by society. With forgiveness and celebration, community becomes the place where we call forth the gifts of other people, lift them up, and say, "You are the beloved daughter and the beloved son."

To celebrate another person's gift doesn't mean giving each other little compliments: "You play the piano better"; "You are so good at singing." No, that's a talent show.

To celebrate each other's gifts means to accept each other's humanity. We see each other as a person who can smile, say "Welcome," eat, and make a few steps. A person who in the eyes of others is broken suddenly is full of life, because you discover your own brokenness through them.

Here is what I mean. In this world, so many people live with the burden of self-rejection: "I'm not good. I'm useless. People don't really care for me. If I didn't have money, they wouldn't talk to me. If I didn't have this big job, they wouldn't call me. If I didn't have this influence, they wouldn't love me." Underneath a successful and highly praised career can live a fearful person who doesn't think much of himself or herself. In community comes that mutual vulnerability in which we forgive each other and celebrate each other's gifts.

I have learned so much since coming to Daybreak. I've learned that my real gifts are not that I write books or that I went to universities. My real gifts are discovered by Janet and Nathan and others who know me so well they cannot be impressed anymore by this other stuff. Once in a while they say, "I have good advice: Why don't you read some of your own books?"

There is healing in being known in my vulnerability and impatience and weakness. Suddenly I realize that Henri is a good person also in the eyes of people who don't read books and who don't care about success. These people can forgive me constantly for the little egocentric gestures and behaviors that are always there.

Ministry

All the disciples of Jesus are called to ministry. Ministry is not, first of all, something that you do (although it calls you to do many things). Ministry is something that you have to trust. If you know you are the beloved, and if you keep forgiving those with whom you form community and celebrate their gifts, you cannot do other than minister.

Jesus cured people not by doing all sorts of complicated things. A power went out from him, and everyone was cured.

He didn't say, "Let me talk to you for ten minutes, and maybe I can do something about this." Everyone who touched him was cured, because a power went out from his pure heart. He wanted one thing—to do the will of God. He was the completely obedient one, the one who was always listening to God. Out of this listening came an intimacy with God that radiated out to everyone Jesus saw and touched.

Ministry means you have to trust that. You have to trust that if you are the son and daughter of God, power will go out from you and that people will be healed.

"Go out and heal the sick. Walk on the snake. Call the dead to life." This is not small talk. Yet Jesus said, "Whatever I do, you can do too and even greater things." Jesus said precisely, "You are sent into the world just as I was sent into the world— to heal, to cure."

Trust in that healing power. Trust that if you are living as the beloved you will heal people whether or not you notice it. But you have to be faithful to that call.

Healing ministry can be expressed in two words: gratitude and compassion.

Healing happens often by leading people to gratitude, for the world is full of resentment. What is resentment? Cold anger. "I'm angry at him. I'm angry at this. This is not the way I want it." Gradually, there are more and more things I am negative about, and soon I become a resentful person.

Resentment makes you cling to your failures or disappointments and complain about the losses in your life. Our life is full of losses—losses of dreams and losses of friends and losses of family and losses of hopes. There is always the lurking danger we will respond to these incredible pains in resentment. Resentment gives us a hardened heart.

Jesus calls us to gratitude. He calls to us, "You foolish people.

Didn't you know that the Son of Man—that you, that we—have to suffer and thus enter into the glory? Didn't you know that these pains were labor pains that lead you to the joy? Didn't you know that all we are experiencing as losses are gains in God's eyes? Those who lose their lives will gain it. And if the grain doesn't die, it stays a small grain; but if it dies, then it will be fruitful."

Can you be grateful for everything that has happened in your life—not just the good things but for all that brought you to today? It was the pain of a Son that created a family of people known as Christians. That's the mystery of God.

Our ministry is to help people to gradually let go of the resentment, to discover that right in the middle of pain there is a blessing. Right in the middle of your tears—that's where the dance starts and joy is first felt.

In this crazy world, there's an enormous distinction between good times and bad, between sorrow and joy. But in the eyes of God, they're never separated. Where there is pain, there is healing. Where there is mourning, there is dancing. Where there is poverty, there is the kingdom.

Jesus says, "Cry over your pains, and you will discover that I'm right there in your tears, and you will be grateful for my presence in your weakness." Ministry means to help people become grateful for life even with pain. That gratitude can send you into the world precisely to the places where people are in pain. The minister, the disciple of Jesus, goes where there is pain not because he is a masochist or she is a sadist, but because God is hidden in the pain.

"Blessed are the poor." Jesus doesn't say, "Blessed are those who care for the poor"; he says, "Blessed are the poor. Blessed are the mourning. Blessed are those who have pain. There I am." To minister, you have to be where the pain is. Sometimes that pain is hidden in a person who from the outside might look painless or successful.

Compassion means to suffer with, to live with those who suffer. When Jesus saw the woman of Nain he realized, "This is a widow who has lost her only son," and he was moved by compassion. He felt the pain of that woman in his guts. He felt her pain so deeply in his spirit that out of compassion he called the son to life so he could give that son back to his mother.

We are sent to wherever there is poverty, loneliness, and suffering to have the courage to be with people. Trust that by throwing yourself into that place of pain you will find the joy of Jesus. All ministries in history are built on that vision. A new world grows out of compassion.

Be compassionate as your heavenly Father is compassionate. It's a great call. But don't be fearful; don't be afraid. Don't say, "I can't do that."

When you are aware that you are the beloved, and when you have friends around you with whom you live in community, you can do anything. You're not afraid anymore. You're not afraid to knock on the door while somebody's dying. You're not afraid to open a discussion with a person who underneath all the glitter is much in need of ministry. You're free.

I've experienced that constantly. When I was depressed or when I felt anxious, I knew my friends couldn't solve it. Those who ministered to me were those who were not afraid to be with me. Precisely where I felt my poverty I discovered God's blessing.

Just a few weeks ago a friend of mine died. He was a classmate, and they sent me the tape of his funeral service. The first reading in that service was a story about a little river. The little river said, "I can become a big river." It worked hard, but there was a big rock. The river said, "I'm going to get around this rock." The little river pushed and pushed, and since it had a lot of strength, it got itself around the rock.

Soon the river faced a big wall, and the river kept pushing this wall. Eventually, the river made a canyon and carved a way through. The growing river said, "I can do it. I can push it. I am not going to give up for anything."

Then there was an enormous forest. The river said, "I'll go ahead anyway and just force these trees down." And the river did that.

The river, now powerful, stood on the edge of an enormous desert with the sun beating down. The river said, "I'm going to go through this desert." But the hot sand soon began to soak up the whole river. The river said, "Oh, no. I'm going to do it. I'm going to get myself through this desert." But the river soon had drained into the sand until it was only a small mud pool.

Then the river heard a voice from above: "Just surrender. Let me lift you up. Let me take over."

The river said, "Here I am."

The sun then lifted up the river and made the river into a huge cloud. He carried the river right over the desert and let the cloud rain down and make the fields far away fruitful and rich.

There is a moment in our life when we stand before the desert and want to do it ourselves. But there is the voice that comes, "Let go. Surrender. I will make you fruitful. Yes, trust me. Give yourself to me."

What counts in your life and mine is not successes but fruits. The fruits of your life you might not see yourself. The fruits of your life are born often in your pain and in your vulnerability and in your losses. The fruits of your life come only after the plow has carved through your land. God wants you to be fruitful.

The question is not, "How much can I still do in the years

that are left to me?" The question is, "How can I prepare myself for total surrender so my life can be fruitful?"

Our little lives are small, human lives. But in the eyes of the One who calls us the beloved, we are great—greater than the years we have. We will bear fruits, fruits that you and I will not see on this earth but in which we can trust.

Solitude, community, ministry—these disciplines help us live a fruitful life. Remain in Jesus; he remains in you. You will bear many fruits, you will have great joy, and your joy will be complete.

Spiritual Formation
and Community

*In this article Henri reflects on the role of spiritual formation
and community in theological education. It originally
appeared in* Sojourners *in August 1977, in an article entitled
"What Do You Know by Heart? Learning Spirituality."*

Recently I read a short story which expresses in a simple
but powerful way the importance of spiritual formation in
theological education. *A little boy was watching a sculptor at
work. For weeks this sculptor kept chipping away at a big block of
marble. After a few weeks he had created a beautiful marble lion.
The little boy was amazed and said: "Mister, how did you know
there was a lion in that rock?*[1]

Long before he knows the marble, the sculptor has to know
the lion. He has to know the lion "by heart" to see him in the

---

[1]Thomas Hora, *Existential Metapsychiatry* (New York: Seabury Press, 1977).

rock. The secret of the sculptor is that what he knows "by heart," he can recognize in the marble. When he knows an angel by heart he will see an angel in the marble, when he knows a demon by heart he will see a demon in the marble, and when he knows God by heart he will see God in the marble. The great question for the sculptor therefore is, "What do you know by heart?"

The story of the boy and the sculptor helps us to see spiritual formation as the formation of the heart. What is the value of a well-trained and well-informed minister when his heart remains ignorant? What is the value of a great theological erudition or a great pastoral adeptness, when there is no well-formed heart to guide a well-informed mind?

Whether the knowledge of the mind leads to God or to the demon depends on the heart. When the word of God remains a subject of analysis and discussion, and does not descend into the heart, it can easily become an instrument of destruction instead of a guide to love. Spiritual formation asks for the ongoing discipline to descend from the mind into the heart so that real knowledge can be found.

Although many people will agree with the need for spiritual formation, the how of it remains for most people a very hard question to answer. It is clear from the many "schools" in the history of Christian spirituality, schools represented by people such as Pseudo-Dionysius the Areopagite, Meister Eckhart, Teresa of Avila, Ignatius Loyola, John Wesley, George Fox, Thomas Merton, the Little Brothers of Jesus, and the brothers of Taize, that there are many ways in spiritual formation. But it is possible to discover underneath this great variety a few themes which can be lifted up as guides for all those who are concerned with their own and other people's spiritual growth. I will concentrate on three themes which seem of special importance in the context of the theological education: *lectio divina*, silence, and guidance.

Lectio Divina

The term *lectio divina* comes from the Benedictine tradition referring to the meditative reading of the Bible. I like to stress the importance of reading the word of God because my growing suspicion is that theological education might unlearn us to read the Bible in the sense of *lectio divina*. Reading the Bible requires first of all approaching the word of God as a word spoken to me, as a word through which God reveals himself to me personally. It is the moment in which my story and God's story meet and in which something must happen. To read the Bible as *lectio divina* means first of all to read "on my knees," reverently, attentively, and with the deep faith that God has a word for me in my own unique situation.

The Bible indeed is not first of all a book of information but of formation, not first of all a book to be analyzed, scrutinized, and discussed, but a book to nurture us, to unify our heart and mind, and to serve as a constant source of contemplation. Only when we are willing to hear the Word as a word for us can the Bible disclose itself and penetrate into the center of our heart. This is far from easy because it requires the constant willingness to be converted and led to places where we rather would not go.

Silence

Without silence the word can never bear fruit. One of the most depressing aspects of contemporary seminaries is the total lack of silence. I have always been impressed by the fact that seminarians, ministers, and priests are such talkative people. Whenever you meet theology students there is a lot of talk.

Often this is a sign of a congenial atmosphere and an open lifestyle, but I wonder if the word of God can really be received in the center of our hearts if the words of his people keep blocking the way.

Silence is the royal road to spiritual formation. I have never met anyone seriously interested in the spiritual life who did not have a growing desire for silence. Not only do those who search for the spirit of truth become growingly aware that "among all the parts of the body the tongue is a whole wicked world in itself" (James 3:6), but they also realize that only through silence will the word of the scriptures be allowed to descend from the mind into the heart. As long as our hearts and minds are filled with words of our own making there simply is no space for the word of God to enter deeply into our heart and bear fruit.

In silence the word of scripture can be received and meditated upon. To meditate therefore means first of all to receive the word of God into our silence where we can ruminate on it, chew on it, "eat it," and let it become flesh and blood in us. Without silence the word cannot become our inner guide because it cannot build its home in our heart and speak from there.

I often wonder if it would not be worthwhile for theology students to spend at least as much time in silent meditation as in the classroom, so that the many words about God they have heard can be sifted out and received into their hearts.

Guidance

Through the Word born out of and always returning to silence the Spirit of God can enter into the heart and cry out from the center of our being. But the road to the heart by Word and silence is not as easy as it seems. We easily get confused, do not know which experiences to trust and which to mistrust, which promptings to follow and which to avoid. The way from the mind to the heart, which is the way of spiritual formation, is not without pitfalls. Therefore, it is not surprising that people who take the spiritual life seriously are always asking for guidance. And in our days many guides are presenting themselves. Sadly enough, there is much amateurism, and only few know the field well enough to be trusted.

One of the most encouraging signs during the last few years is the development of centers where people are trained in spiritual direction. There is a growing need for people who can help in the task to distinguish the Holy Spirit from many unholy spirits. My guess is that the future of theological education will be significantly influenced by this new development. When students are deeply concerned to create space for the liberating power of the Holy Spirit in their innermost self, then studies in exegesis, dogmatics, ethics, history, and especially pastoral care will have significantly increased heart-forming potential.

Whatever the specific "school of prayer" we are dealing with, each stresses that the word of God needs to be received in silence under the eye of a competent guide. But still this is not the final word on spiritual formation. It can even be quite deceptive since it might suggest that spiritual formation is a highly individual affair. I read the word, I enter in silence, and I talk with a specialist to help me in my way to the heart. Spiritual formation is easily perceived as the training of spiritual giants, and then quickly the idea develops that special spiritual seekers are guided by special spiritual masters in the application of special spiritual techniques and methods. Here we touch on a difference in emphasis between Christian spirituality and the Asian spiritualities.

Community

Christian spirituality is in essence communal. The prayer life of the Christian can never be understood independent of community life. Prayer in the Christian life leads to community, and community to prayer. *Lectio divina*, silence, and guidance come to full fruition in the context of the Christian community. Therefore, the reading of the word of God and silent listening to it are not individual techniques leading to individual perfection. The spiritual director is not a guru whose authority depends on his personal enlightenment. They all are an integral part of the life of the people of God which expresses itself first and foremost in corporate worship.

Our temptation is to understand the formation of the heart as a highly individual affair. This temptation of individualism is particularly strong when seminaries and divinity schools are part of highly ambitious and competitive academic institutions. Wherever ambition and competition are dominant, the formation of community is extremely difficult if not impossible. And still ministry means first of all service to the people of God and can never be reduced to psychiatric or psychological models in which the one-to-one relationship is central. All of this suggests strongly that spiritual formation in theological education includes ongoing formation in community life.

The word is first of all read in community, silence is first of all part of our life together, and spiritual direction should first of all be seen and experienced as direction in the name of the larger community.

If this is true, many new questions arise, not just in terms of the content and method of theological education but even more in terms of its style. Do we as students and teachers experience theological education as a communal responsibility? Do we fully realize that we are called to learn together with each other, from each other, and supported by each other? Is the classroom a place of communal life, and are projects, papers, and fieldwork indeed growing out of our life together? Are daily worship and weekly communion the culmination and fullest expression of our experience as the people of God?

All these and similar questions are of great importance if we really believe that ministry is primarily a vocation given by and performed in the name of the community. Theology students are not prepared for such a ministry when everything they experienced during their formal education encouraged them to be competitive and highly individualistic.

Let us not fool ourselves by thinking that spiritual formation can be possible in a highly privatized milieu. It might in fact have the opposite effect. When word, silence, and guidance as ways to the heart are introduced into a basically individualistic milieu, they might simply feed our narcissistic tendencies and lead to a spiritual self-centeredness. Then so-called "spiritual formation" leads to small-heartedness and moves us away from the biblical call to be shepherds of the people of God. It is therefore quite understandable that wherever authentic spiritual growth takes place there is always a strengthening of community, and that wherever authentic community is found there always is a growing desire for a deepening of the spiritual life.

But let me add quickly here that community has little or nothing to do with contemporary "group techniques." Small group discussions, dialogues in class, sensitivity workshops, and all other ways of bringing people closer together are not necessarily an expression of community. The opposite might quite well be true. People who have been in a training group

("T-group") for a whole year may learn a lot about leadership patterns or human interaction, but they do not necessarily form community.

Community is a gift of the Spirit which can express itself in many very different ways: in silence as well as in words, in listening as well as in speaking, in living together as well as in solitary life, and in many ways of worship. Community itself is foremost a quality of the heart which enables us to unmask the illusion of our competitive society and recognize each other as brothers and sisters in Christ and sons and daughters of the same Father. As a quality of the heart, community is not bound to any particular institutional form but is free to create new forms of living wherever it manifests itself.

So spiritual life is always communal. It flows from community and it creates community. It is the life of the Spirit in us, the Spirit of God who dwells in the center of our hearts and in the center of our lives together. That which is most personal proves to be most communal; that which is most intimate proves to be most public; and that which is most nourishing for our individual lives proves to be the best food for our lives as the people of God. It is therefore not surprising that prayer and community are always found together, because the same Spirit who prays in us is the Spirit who binds us together into one body.

How can we articulate the importance of spiritual formation for contemporary ministers? The best way seems to be to consider the way to the heart as the way to freedom. It is the way to freedom because it is the way to the truth and the truth will set us free. When Jesus left his disciples he said: "It is for your own good that I am going, because unless I go, the Advocate will not come to you; but if I do go, I will send him to you. . . . He will lead you to the complete truth" (John 16:7–13).

The Spirit of Truth liberates us from our ignorance, which

keeps us enslaved. Ignorance makes us look for acceptance where it cannot be found and makes us hope for changes where they cannot be expected. Ignorance makes us fight for a new world as if we can do it ourselves and makes us judge our neighbors as if we have the final word. Ignorance keeps us entangled in the illusions of our world and causes us to suffer many pains and sorrows.

The spiritual life is a life by which we are set free by the Spirit of God, which is the Spirit of Truth. By this Spirit we can indeed be *in* the world without being *of* it. We can move freely without being bound by false attachments. We can speak freely without fear of human rejection. And we can live with peace and joy even when surrounded by conflict and many sadnesses. It was that Spirit that set the disciples free to travel great distances and speak boldly the word of God even when it led to persecution, imprisonment, and death. It is that same Spirit which will give us the freedom to live in our death-oriented society as witnesses to the new life which has come in and through Jesus Christ.

Spiritual formation is an indispensable part of theological education. It prepares us for a life in which we are free from the compulsions and needs born out of ignorance and free to serve in the world even when this leads us to places where we rather would not go. Spiritual formation gives us a free heart able to see the face of God in the midst of a hardened world and allows us to use our skills to make that face visible to all who live in darkness.

3

Finding Solitude
in Community

In this article Henri discusses the urgency of solitude for Christian communities that are at risk of burnout, exploring common misunderstandings and offering guidance for communities to find a healthy rhythm. It appeared originally in Worship *magazine in 1978.*

Today many people who live in community are asking themselves, "How do I find time and space for myself?" This question, which can arise in almost any kind of community, becomes even more understandable when we realize that many of the communities now in existence were born in response to a growing awareness of such destructive forces in our contemporary society as racial discrimination, oppression of the poor, the proliferation of nuclear arms, and the plight of political prisoners.

These new communities are discernible by the fact that in them new ways of living are directly connected with service to the poor, oppressed, and downtrodden. Yet the people to whom these communities want to be of service often have so many urgent needs that time and space to pray, to read, to write, or just to be alone seem nearly impossible to attain. Those who have been living in such "prophetic" communities are therefore beginning to wonder how they can preserve themselves from physical, mental, and spiritual exhaustion. How can they find some solitude in which to reanimate inner vitality, discover new perspectives, and stay in touch with their own inner resources?

In the recent past, the intensity of life together has caused some members to withdraw from their communities for varying periods of time and others to leave permanently. Several communities were unable to sustain themselves and dissolved after long, painful struggles. We are dealing here with one of the most important questions of community life. It is the question of the place of solitude in life together.

The question is often phrased in very concrete ways: "Where can I find an hour to read undisturbed? How can I avoid constantly being bombarded by demands and requests?" This search for solitude also reveals itself in such familiar complaints as, "There are always thousands of things going on here; you can hardly keep up with them!" From these questions and complaints specific desires are born: "I often dream about a whole day just for myself, but it probably will never be possible as long as we live here together surrounded by so many pains and needs. It even sounds like asking for a luxury!" Such questions, complaints, and dreams cluster around the deep human need for solitude.

It is becoming increasingly apparent that for the long-term survival of a community solitude is essential. Without solitude, life together is doomed to fail. This is true for every form of life together—marriage, friendship, and small-group living. It is especially important, however, for all communities which consider themselves prophetic communities or communities of resistance. Precisely because these communities represent such crucial voices in our society, it is of utmost importance that they themselves receive the nurture and care which only solitude can offer.

In the following pages I want to offer some reflections on solitude in community in the hope that for some communities these ideas may offer new strength to remain faithful to the vision which originally brought them together. These reflections have been shaped through discussions with numerous friends who live in community and who are deeply concerned about the destructive and often suicidal tendencies in our world. They are written with the desire to help these communities avoid becoming "burned-out cases" which have lost the spiritual power to be sources of hope in the midst of a chaotic world.

I will start by describing two commonly held viewpoints on the role of solitude in community which I consider false or at least too limited. Then I will try to articulate in a more positive way the indispensable place of solitude in life together. It is my hope that these observations will stimulate further discussion of this topic among those who have heard the great call to community.

Two Familiar Viewpoints

Solitude Over Against Community

There is a distinction prevalent in many circles between time for oneself and time for the community. As soon as we make that distinction we have created a battle between the concerns of the individual and the concerns of the community. Once the lines are thus drawn, an endless number of false preoccupations develop.

Solitude in whatever form then becomes an individual right over against the rights of the community. This distinction places solitude in the sphere of "private life," which is seen in opposition to "life together." Solitude is the time and space in which I can be myself, do my thing, work on that part of my life that is for me and me alone. Once we allow ourselves to be drawn into this way of thinking, we have accepted a false and very dangerous dichotomy which can affect our thoughts, feelings, and behavior in an extremely destructive way.

One of the main effects of this view of solitude is that those with whom I have chosen to live my life become also those whom I consider my rivals. They share my most personal concerns, but they also threaten to take away my most precious privacy. They give me opportunities to realize my ideals, but they also prevent my personal growth. They give me much care, but they also claim that part of me that is exclusively my own.

Those who adhere to this dichotomy identify solitude with "privacy" and therefore consider it to be in competition with life in community. But this perspective is seductive because it conceals a very "worldly" way of thinking. It gives the status of undeniable truth to claims such as "I have a right to privacy" and "Time for oneself is a basic human need." There is a misleading viewpoint operating in these claims which can cause much unnecessary suffering.

For instance, it can create guilt feelings because our desire for solitude is experienced as a desire for time away from those with whom we promised to live together. When we want silence, time to study, pray, read, or write, we often feel guilty because we know there are so many more urgent and more important things to do. This misleading viewpoint also gives rise to irritability.

We experience the demands others make on our time as attacks on our personal needs and obey outwardly while resisting from within. This viewpoint also causes inner tension and nervousness. When we do claim some time and space for ourselves, we still may find it hard really to profit from it: our awareness of the call of the others to join them in their work keeps our heart restless and confused.

There is always something to do. How can we be at peace with ourselves when we feel that our friends need us? Guilt feelings, irritability, inner tensions, nervousness, and many other forms of suffering can be the result of a false dichotomy between solitude and community and can cause great harm to our life together.

Solitude in Service of Community

There is a second view of solitude which I consider false or at least very limited. It is the view in which solitude becomes merely a tool in the service of life together. Solitude is no longer time and space for the individual in contrast to time and space for the community, but simply a function of the community. Solitude is good for the members of the community because they can return from it refreshed, restored, and better able to engage in the common task.

The positive side of this view of solitude is that it prevents solitude from becoming identical with privacy and connects it more closely with community living. But the negative side of this perspective is that it reduces solitude to a place of healing from which we may reenter the fullness of life together. Although solitude and community are no longer separated as rivals, there is still a distance. This distance can be felt in remarks such as, "I really need a little time for myself so that I can get myself together again," or "Everyone needs some time away from the busy life of every day to get centered again." These remarks illustrate how solitude is equated with a place of restoration, re-creation, and integration in which we gather new forces for our life together.

It is true that solitude can offer healing to our wounded self, and we may indeed return from solitude more vital and more energetic, but to believe that this is the primary role of solitude leads to false ideas. It can lead, for example, to the idea that solitude is the refuge of the weak. "The strong don't need it and those who ask for it are in bad shape and need to be restored." It also leads to the idea that solitude is subservient to life in community. Solitude becomes a means to an end: "We all need solitude because from time to time we all are weak, but what really matters is our life and work together."

Most importantly it leads to the idea that the need for solitude is only temporary: "Solitude is good for us once in a while—in special situations, under special stress, when there is too much stimulation or too much distraction. But when things are normal, solitude is no longer necessary and all our energy can be spent for our time together." In many people's minds, time alone to pray or play and time away from the unceasing stream of new stimuli is like a therapeutic device, a mere means to regain one's strength for the battlefield. It is my deep conviction that this view of solitude, no less than the view which identifies solitude with privacy, will slowly paralyze community life and eventually kill the most vital forces of life together. Therapeutic periods of solitude might be sufficient for short-term life together, but for people with long-term commitments to community occasional solitude is not enough.

We are now in a position to ask about the relationship between solitude and community. Solitude is not a private space over against the public space of community, nor is it merely a healing space in which we restore ourselves for community life. Solitude and community belong together; each requires the other as do the center and circumference of a circle. Solitude without community leads us to loneliness and despair, but community without solitude hurls us into a "void of words and feelings" (Bonhoeffer).

I now would like to develop this view in more detail by relating solitude to intimacy, clarity, and prayer. Hopefully this will lead us to a better insight into the dynamic unity of solitude and community.

Solitude and Intimacy

Solitude is essential to community life because in solitude we grow closer to each other. When we pray alone, study, read, write, or simply spend quiet time away from the places where we interact with each other directly, we are in fact participating fully in the growth of community. It is a fallacy to think that we grow closer to each other only when we talk, play, or work together. Much growth certainly occurs in such human interactions, but at least as much growth can take place when we enter into solitude. We take the other with us into solitude, and there the relationship grows and deepens. In solitude we discover each other in a way which physical presence makes difficult, if not impossible. There we recognize a bond with each other that does not depend on words, gestures, or actions and that is deeper and stronger than our own efforts can create.

If we base our life together on our physical proximity, on our ability to spend time together, speak with each other, eat together, and worship together, community life soon will become demanding and tiring. Only when all these activities are experienced and lived as an expression of a deeper unity can they remain free and open. Solitude is indeed essential to genuine community. There we grow closer to each other because there we can encounter the source of our unity.

One way to express this is to say that in solitude we are given the awareness of a unity that is prior to all unifying actions. It is the place where we come to realize that we were together before we came together and that community life is not a creation of human will but an obedient response to the reality of our being united. Every time we affirm that solitude belongs to the essence of life together, we express our faith in a love which transcends our interpersonal communication and proclaim that we love each other because we have first been loved (1 Jn 4:19).

Solitude means to surrender ourselves to that greater love and to rest in the safe embrace of him whose faithfulness lasts from age to age (Ps 118). Although this might sound too "mystical" or too "unpractical," it is meant to be a very pragmatic observation. Many people who have lived together for years and whose love for one another has been tested more than once know that the decisive experience in their life was not that they were able to hold together but that they were held together. Solitude is the ongoing return to this sustaining love from which the community draws its strength.

In the actual life of the community, this means that it cannot be left to individual members to decide upon and deal with solitude. When a community in effect says to its members, "Everyone should try to find some solitude for himself or for herself," then the community is not really in touch with its own reality. Solitude is so central to life together that a community is responsible for structuring it in such a way that it ceases to be simply a day-to-day decision of the individual and becomes instead part of the daily rhythm of life together. Time for silence, individual study, and personal prayer and meditation must be of as much importance to all the members of the community as eating together, working together, playing together, and worshiping together.

I am deeply convinced that gentleness, tenderness, peacefulness, and the inner freedom to move closer to one another or to withdraw from one another are nurtured in solitude. Without solitude, we begin to cling to each other, we begin to worry about what we think and feel about each other, and we begin, often in an unconscious way, to scrutinize each other with a tiring hypersensitivity. With solitude we learn to depend on God, by whom we are called together in love, in whom we can rest and through whom we can enjoy and trust one another even when our ability to express ourselves to each other is limited.

Without solitude, shallow conflicts easily grow deep and cause painful wounds. Then "talking things out" becomes a burdensome obligation, and daily life becomes so self-conscious that long-term living together is virtually impossible. With solitude we are preserved from the most pernicious effects of our mutual suspicions. Our words and actions can then be a joyful expression of an already existing trust rather than a subtle way of asking for proof of a trusting relationship.

Without solitude we will always suffer from gnawing questions about more and less: "Does he love me more than she? Is our love today less than it was yesterday?" These questions lead to divisions, tensions, apprehensions, and mutual irritability. With solitude we are no longer compelled to raise such questions continuously, but can experience each other as different manifestations of a love which transcends all of us. Thus solitude is essential to life together. It is not a place in which we can hide out or merely a place of healing. Rather, it is the place in which we come together more intimately than we could through any particular words or gestures.

Solitude and Clarity

Another way to express the necessity of solitude in community is to call it the way to clarity. In solitude we begin to see more clearly and are more able to distinguish between what can be shared and what should be left unspoken. Solitude helps us to reevaluate the notion that we should share and work through with each other all that crowds our minds and hearts. We are living in a time marked by an almost limitless faith in the value of interpersonal expression. The result of this is that we tend to spend many hours exploring our most personal ideas and feelings about ourselves and each other. Of course it is often of great value to establish a confessing and forgiving relationship with one another, but we must not underestimate the limits of our ability fully to communicate ourselves to each other.

Many who have sought peace and tranquility through the sharing of their innermost experiences have found themselves entangled in an increasing sense of loneliness. Often the desired catharsis failed to occur and in its place there arose feelings of disappointment and even resentment. The reason for such experiences, it seems to me, is that we have been misled into believing that we possess the psychic tools to create or restore our life together through the uninhibited expression of our pains and joys. But precisely here we are fooling ourselves.

Community is not a human creation but a divine gift which calls for an obedient response. This response may require much patience and humility, much listening and speaking, much confrontation and self-examination, but it should always be an obedient response to a bond which is given and not made.

In this perspective solitude receives a very special meaning; it helps us to avoid using, overusing, or misusing each other. It helps us present our deepest human struggles to God and to discover in silence that we are accepted in a way and to a degree which transcend the possibilities of human interaction. Each time we enter into solitude and present ourselves to God with all our anxieties and joys, doubts and certainties, wounds and talents, a deepening sense of acceptance can grow in us, an acceptance which sets us free from interpersonal compulsions. This sense of basic acceptance prevents us from expecting of the members of the community more understanding than they can provide, more affection than they can offer, more insight than they have, and more care than they can show, and enables us to receive the many gifts of the community in joyful gratitude. So solitude gives us a clear eye for God's unconditional love and for the many human gifts through which we can receive it.

This has very concrete implications for our interpersonal relationships. Often, when we are filled with inner tensions, concerns, and needs and feel a strong impulse to express them to the community, it may be of great importance to spend some time in silence before sharing our concerns. In this silence we can bring our fears into perspective and allow our expectations of support and help from others to become more realistic. I wonder if many counseling sessions would not be much more fruitful and creative if they were started with a period of shared silence.

Silence is an element of solitude that can be introduced into our daily life without great effort. When members of a community begin to experience silence as part of all they do—eating, working, playing, and praying—then the words will be heard better and received more deeply. Through silence a little bit of our solitude can enter into the midst of our actions and keep us in the remembrance of the Lord who brings us together. It is this easily available solitude that prevents us from being cluttered, confused, clinging, and needy, and keeps our heart and mind clear and open. It helps us to distinguish carefully between what can be creatively shared with others and what is best understood in the silence of our own heart.

Solitude and Prayer

A third way of looking at the central place of solitude in the life of the community is to consider it from the perspective of prayer. I have presupposed this perspective throughout the discussions of intimacy and clarity. Now I would like to bring it into the foreground. When I speak of prayer I refer less to saying prayers than to living a prayerful life in which eating and drinking, sleeping and waking, working and praying are all done to the honor and glory of God. In solitude life is affirmed as prayer. We can say a thousand times to ourselves and to each other that community is not the result of human effort and we can remind ourselves and each other in many ways that God is the source of our life together, but without solitude this conviction tends to remain merely verbal. In solitude we detach ourselves from immediate, goal-oriented actions and from the many words by which we try to make ourselves understood, and stand before God empty-handed.

In solitude we can be "useless" for a while and learn not simply with our head but also with our heart that community is a gift to which we should respond in gratitude. The Russian Orthodox monk Theophan the Recluse defines prayer as standing in the presence of God with our mind in our heart. It is in solitude that our knowledge of God can indeed descend from our mind into our heart and thus become the focus of our life together.

It is far from easy to affirm not only with our mind but with our whole heart that we are a community not because we like each other or have a common task or project, but because we are called together by God. God, not psychological similarities or social circumstances, is our bond. In solitude we affirm and celebrate this joyful fact. It is joyful because it frees us from false concerns and anxieties and so liberates us from an unrewarding preoccupation with human interactions.

The psychiatrist Thomas Hora sees real community symbolized by two hands coming together and pointing upward in a prayerful position. In his view community is a joint participation in a love greater than we ourselves can contain or express. When we rely on the strength of our interpersonal relationships as the basis for community we become, as Hora sees it, like interlocking fingers which stalemate each other and lose their freedom of movement.[1] Solitude is inseparable from community because in solitude we affirm the deepest reality of our lives together, namely, that as a community we are like hands pointing to God in prayer. We might even say that community life itself is first of all a prayerful gesture. People do not form community when they cling to each other in order to survive the storms of the world, but they do form community when together they erect a living prayer in the midst of our anxiety-ridden human family.

All this suggests that life in solitude is a life in faith. By leaving behind from time to time our many self-affirming actions and becoming "useless" in the presence of God, we transcend

---

[1] Thomas Hora, *Existential Metapsychiatry* (New York: Seabury Press, 1977), 31–38.

our inner fears and apprehensions and affirm our God as the one in whose love we find our strength and security.

This viewpoint has some concrete implications. It leads to the convictions that worship together, although extremely important for the life of the community, should not be the only form of prayer. It is crucial for the long-term life of a community that the members continuously encourage one another to spend time alone with God. When the total worship life of a community is focused on the common periods of prayer, it is tempting to rely too much upon the supportive atmosphere of common prayers and to expect too much from the warmth and gentleness of shared songs, silences, and prayers. There are times when we must dare to be alone with God and to find our real identity there. This might be difficult and painful but it is a real service to our life together. After all, a house is stronger when the pillars on which it rests do not depend on each other but have their own separate foundations.

This brings me to the end of these reflections on solitude and community. It certainly will not be easy to give solitude the central place it deserves in community life. There are many forces which pull us away from it, especially the often all-pervasive mood of urgency and emergency. But when we think about community as a way of living rather than an expedient tactic for specific situations, solitude cannot remain absent very long.

Without solitude, a prophetic community loses its pastoral dimension and soon extinguishes its own light. With solitude, community can withstand many storms and even live creatively in times when there are no urgent calls to move outward into action. Solitude enables the community to breathe in as well as to breathe out and gives it a healthy rhythm.

How can we more fully integrate solitude into our life together? It would seem that understanding the essential role of solitude is a necessary beginning. The absence of real solitude is often the result of a lack of insight into its importance. When we shake off the biases which lead us to think of solitude as an escape or withdrawal from community and rediscover solitude as the necessary counterpart to community, then our heart may be willing to follow our mind. We may then find the strength to oppose the many forces which push us back into fragmentation and alienation.

Education to solitude, therefore, is an important task for communities of resistance. It helps the community to discover its own reality and so strengthens it in its primary task. When solitude is given its rightful place, communities will be able to resist not only the flagrantly visible ills of our society, but also the evils whose roots reach into the depth of our being and threaten the life of our community itself.

4

The Faces of Community

In this article, published in the Catholic Worker *newspaper in 1978, Henri discusses how finding and forming community requires a radical conversion of heart and mind to the way of Christ.*

There is little doubt that in our competitive world much emphasis is placed on those aspects of our personality which make us stand out. The thousands of advertisements that bombard us every day inform us of the outstanding quality of their products. The sports reporters who speak to us in daily papers and through radio and TV call our attention to the outstanding performances of their heroes, and when we go to a play, a movie, or a circus to be entertained, we quickly focus on the outstanding activities of the artists. This emphasis on what is "outstanding" is so pervasive that we are hardly aware of how much it influences our emotions, passions, and feelings. But when we stop for a moment and reflect on the way we perceive ourselves and our neighbors, we soon discover how much of our energy is invested in comparing ourselves with others and wondering how we are special and where we stand out.

Maybe during the first six years of our lives we are still able simply to enjoy life as it comes to us and to respond spontaneously to our surroundings. As soon as we go to school, however, we begin to ask the fatal question: "Am I doing better or am I doing worse than my classmates?" From then on we find ourselves struggling for grades, prizes, and other special rewards for our accomplishments. In this context, it is not surprising that our sense of self, our self-esteem begins to depend increasingly on those aspects of our life in which we are different from others. We wonder if we are more or less smart, fast, handsome, or practical than others, and our vocabulary quickly becomes full of comparative terms. The more we allow this way of thinking to dominate our lives, the more we become victims of the grade-givers in our society and succumb to the illusion that we are the difference we make.

It is not hard to see that this emphasis on the "outstanding" prevents us from forming community. Concerned with maintaining our differences, we live in constant fear that someone might take them from us and so undermine our sense of well-being. And so we start clinging anxiously to what we have: our possessions, which set us apart from others; our skills and techniques, by which we can do what others cannot do; our insights, by which we can impress people; and even our spiritual experiences, which give us a sense of being special. Learning then becomes a battlefield in which people try to get for themselves that which allows them to stand out and make a difference.

Entering the Human Condition

The gospel radically criticizes this way of living and thinking. The great news of the gospel is that self-identification based on outstanding differences makes us competitive and violent people who hold on compulsively to our distinctions and defend them at all costs. Jesus Christ reveals to us that our real identity is not to be found on the edges of our existence where we can brag about our specialties, but in the center where we can recognize our basic human sameness and discover each other as brothers and sisters, children of the same God.

This is not a theoretical statement made by Christ, but a reality made visible in the life of Christ himself. The great mystery of revelation is indeed that Jesus Christ did not cling to his equality with God but emptied himself and became as we are. He revealed himself not in being different from us but in being one with us, in sharing our joys and pains and dying a human death. This is very hard for us to understand fully, but we need to keep trying to stay close to this most profound mystery of God's love. God showed his love for us not by taking away our pains and frustrations and erasing our difficulties, but by becoming part of our human condition and living as we do.

What is central here is that by accepting the human condition God in no way became less than God but, on the contrary revealed to us what his being God for us really means. He revealed to us that it belongs to the essence of his nature that he does not keep distant, but enters with us into the human struggle. Based on this understanding of God as a God with us, the Apostle Paul could say to the Philippians: "There must be no competition among you, no conceit; but everybody is to be self-effacing. Always consider the other person to be better than yourself, so that nobody thinks of his own interests first but everybody thinks of other people's interest instead. In your minds you must be the same as Christ Jesus" (Philippians 2:3–5).

To live the Christian life therefore requires a radical conversion. It requires us to look for our identity not where we are different or outstanding but where we are the same. This is far from easy because it requires us to give up many cherished illusions and to face directly our real human condition. It seems realistic to say that we have such deep fears and are filled with so many doubts and insecurities that facing our own broken human condition is beyond our own strength. However, it is also realistic to say that the love of God made visible in Jesus Christ can open for us the road to a new identity based not on our differences but on the full recognition of our human sameness.

It is the experience of the unconditional love of God that allows us to recognize our common human brokenness and our common need for healing. When we are pervaded by fear, we cannot be self-effacing or consider the other person as better than ourselves. That would be mental suicide. But when we are liberated from fear by God's unlimited love, then we can give up our illusions and live out our human sameness with great freedom.

One of the most remarkable aspects of the lives of the saints is that the closer they came to a full understanding of God, the closer they came to being human. The more they experienced God's love in their life, the more they became aware of their own sinfulness and brokenness, and stressed that they were no different from others. This has nothing to do with masochism, self-flagellation, or false humility, but it is an expression of the knowledge that in the full recognition of the broken human condition our true identity finds its anchor-place.

Community

All this makes it clear that living according to the gospel, living with the mind of Christ, leads to community. Whereas a life based on our differences makes us strangers to each other, a life based on our common human brokenness and our common need for healing brings us closer to each other and so encourages community. Community starts becoming visible as soon as we perceive ourselves as fellow travelers, as people on the same road.

It seems important to stress here that community is not so much something we create after we have given up our defensiveness and competitiveness. Rather, it becomes a reality when we relate to each other according to our true identity.

Secondly, it is important not to limit too soon our concept of community. One tends to think immediately of people living together in one house or forming some kind of life together. But a classroom can be a community. People coming together for worship can form community. People writing to each other can be in community. Teachers, health care workers, and people in different professions can all form community. It all depends on the way we come to each other. Human beings are created for each other, and are alive to give and share. As this truth becomes the basis of action, and as the paralyzing fears and isolating divisions begin to dissolve, community again becomes visible, revealing itself as natural, obvious, and self-evident.

It is in community that people begin to discover each other's uniqueness. Community is the place where talents can be discovered and made fruitful. Here we touch the great paradox of sameness and uniqueness. When we are willing to give up our outstanding differences and come to each other in mutual vulnerability, aware of our basic human sameness, then we create a space in which individual talents can manifest themselves not as divisive qualities but as uniting gifts.

On the common ground of shared brokenness, our gifts can reveal themselves as gifts for each other. The most remarkable aspect of Christian community is that it does not encourage uniformity and suppress individual gifts. On the contrary, it creates the milieu in which, through great attentiveness to each other, hidden talents are brought to the foreground and made available for the upbuilding of communal life. Precisely when we have discovered that our sense of self does not depend on our differences and that our self-esteem is based on a love much deeper than the praise which can be acquired by unusual performances, we can see our own unique talents as gifts for others. And then we realize that the sharing of our gifts does not diminish our own value as persons but enhances it.

In community, the unique talents of the individual members become like the little stones which form a great mosaic. The fact that the little piece of gold is part of a brilliant mural makes it that much more important since it is now an essential part of a greater picture. When this becomes clear, then our dominant attitude toward each other's gifts becomes gratitude. With increasing clarity we see the beauty in each other and call it forth so that it may become a part of our total life together. With increasing confidence we expect God's love to become visible in new ways through those who dare to meet on the common ground of their humanity. So sameness and uniqueness can both be affirmed in community.

We need to recognize the illusion that we are the difference we make and come together on the basis of our sameness. Indeed, we must have the desire to live out this sameness to the fullest. We have to experience our humanity to the core, our brokenness as well as our need for God's healing grace. But above all, we must realize that it is right in the center of this sameness that we will discover the gifts we have to share and the talents we can offer each other.

5

Called from Darkness

In this address at a worship service in New York City marking the United Nations General Assembly's Second Special Session on Disarmament in 1982, Henri discusses the importance of prayer, resistance, and community in peacemaking.

"I have told you these things so that in me you may have peace. In this world you will have trouble, but take heart, I have overcome the world" (John 16:33).

Brothers and Sisters, I would very much like to share with you a few reflections about a spirituality of peacemaking. I'd like you to consider three words. The first word is prayer. The second word is resistance. And the third word is community. Consider these three words in the light of the words of Jesus from John's Gospel: "So that in me you may have peace." This has something to do with prayer. "In this world you will have trouble"—the causes for resistance. "But take heart, I have overcome the world." And that is what we want to celebrate and what we want to affirm in our life together in community.

Prayer, resistance, and community can help sustain us in our movement and pursuit of peace.

Prayer

First, a word about prayer. I don't know if it has happened to you, but to me it happened quite recently that suddenly I became deeply aware that a lot of my actions, a lot of the things I was doing came forth out of my needs, and my needs quite often were related to deep, deep hurts that somewhere were hidden far away in my own history. I had a need for affection. A need for attention. A need for popularity. A need for power. And somewhere those needs were deeply rooted in my life and came forth out of moments when I might have been rejected, with or without the knowledge of those who did so.

But somewhere I started to realize that often I'd been longing for attention and affection and popularity and success and I was going around doing a lot of good things, but those were coming out of that need. And then I found that there were a lot of other people who had the same need and responded to me with that need, and so needs started to intermingle with needs, and slowly I realized how interdependent and sucking and clinging and sticky many of my relationships and works were which I tended to call . . . "ministry." And, quite honestly, I was shocked by that realization.

While I was thinking and doing a lot of things in the name of the kingdom of God, I was deeply involved in a domain of Satan himself who just was playing all those games with me. "Do this! Do that! Because otherwise you might not be loved." And I started to see that when I act out of needs and out of those hurts, quite often without me wanting it, I find myself involved in the fruits of the demon which is resentment, anger, violence, greed. When I saw that not only in me but around me, I started to realize how many conflicts and wars are in fact connected with those unresolved human needs that go so deep in our psyche and so deep all the way back into history—from the fathers to the fathers, from the mothers to the mothers— somewhere we are in that needy reality.

Now prayer is that slow process which we move away from that dark place of our needs into the light of Christ. Into the light that allows us to act not out of those needs and those fears and those pains, but out of a new freedom. Prayer is to stop breathing that sticky, sweaty, polluted air and to start breathing with the breath of God, the air of God, the breath by which we are created and the breath by which we are able to cry out "Abba. Father!" Praying leads us to that place in us where we can be in touch with that renewing spirit and can act not out of our needs, not out of our hurts, but where we can act out of that new life that has entered into us. And the fruits are very clear. The fruits are joy, peace, freedom, gentleness, tenderness, care, and real creative human relationships.

Brothers and Sisters, I am saying this because I feel that it's so important for us to realize that prayer in this sense of entering into that inner dwelling place where the spirit of God lives, prayer is indeed the beginning of all peacemaking. Peacemaking therefore might not be first of all to do many things, to get very involved, but to first of all resist all those powers that subdue us and to come to that quiet place where we can realize that we are not the attention we are getting, that we are not the affection we are receiving, that we are not the power we have, or the popularity we receive, but that we are truly a manifestation of God's love. That long before we could love or do or think anything, we were loved by him. And to pray is to come in touch with that first love and to really experience that.

Prayer as an Act of Resistance

Prayer is really an act of resistance—resistance against this needy, sucking, and frightening merry-go-round. First of all we must believe that there is a power of love in us stronger and deeper than we have ever dared to realize. And therefore exactly in this time when so much is happening, when there is so much restlessness and so much anger and confusion, it is of incredible importance that you *dare* to resist that and sit down, wait, listen, and be silent. Listen to the word of God in you and to reflect on those psalms and think about those readings from the prophets and evangelists. Slowly allow those words to descend from your mind into your heart so that you can experience that power of peace in you, so that when you go out and move you are not doing it because you need it so much, but because you feel this abundance of love that you want to share.

Realize that prayer is an act of resistance. An act that leads to freedom. For the second word is the word "resistance." There is no question in my mind, and I don't think in yours, that resistance indeed is essential for all the ways of peacemaking. Resistance means to say, "No! No! No!" against all the forces of death. That's what resistance is: to say no to death. And that is a very, very hard task, because it simply does not only mean to say no to the nuclear arms by which we now can commit collective suicide, but it also means to say no to death that pervades much of our life all the time. Films, movies, novels, and books, all around we see something that frightens me personally more and more, a certain kind of fascination with death and darkness. To resist that is an enormous, hard, Christian, human task. There are subtle influences that must be resisted. You say, "I don't like that person and I'm not going to like him ever. I know what kind of guy he is." And suddenly things are fixed into a relationship that seeks not life, but death. "I am no longer going to believe that anything is really going to change in this world." "I've seen enough. You can't tell me anything, all those sentimentalities about a better future and all that. I don't want to hear anything about that anymore."

That resentment, you feel the coldness of it. Something is stuck there and doesn't move anymore. That's death. Or it's like spending all those hours around the table and we are just complaining about everybody else. We can sit and spend hours of our time playing with death in our hearts, because we feel sort of excited about talking about things that titillate us and give us a sense of being in control and having a certain way of controlling our existence by deciding what is good and what is bad. That is death's work, not work for peace. It is the work of the demon in our hearts, in our society, and in our communities.

We want things to be so clear that we prefer the security of misery above the insecurity of happiness. What are we going to do when we have nothing to complain about anymore? When we have no terrible movies to see and we cannot sit there and tremble because of all those dangerous things that are happening, and when there is nobody against us anymore? What happens when we have no enemies to fight, when we have no people to gossip about? What are we going to do?

Suddenly we start to realize that in that situation we could see the first signs of change. And we don't want everything to change. We want to know what's happening. We want to stay in control. We want to say this is this, and that is that, and let's just keep it that way. To really believe that life is what we have to entrust ourselves to, means that you and I have to entrust ourselves continually to change. Life is in constant movement, always changing. Change confounds our expectations. If you want to fix life, you make it die and it sits there. And so we have to say "No" to the forces of death wherever we find them, and in unexpected places. You are not a peacemaker if you don't say "No" to the small things, as well as the big ones. That's not peacemaking. Resistance is not just simply saying "No." In fact, I think it's more saying "Yes!"

Resistance in the deepest sense means to continuously proclaim that God is a God of the living, that God is a God of life. What we are called to do first of all is to say "Yes" to life and to the God of life. Because I tell you, if you are too preoccupied with saying "No!" you might get tainted by the forces you say "No" to. We can fight so hard against issues that we become hostile, angry peacemakers. We can become like the violence we are fighting against, resentful, bitter, violent peacemakers. There are thousands of them around. It is very important for us to realize that everyone who directly attacks evil always tends to become tainted by it. I know that from myself and you know it too. You get involved in things you are against and suddenly you are as dark as the forces you are against. And so I think that saying "No" has to be always subservient to saying "Yes," because "Yes" is really what sets us free.

The God of the Living

The essence of the Christian message is that God is a God of the living. That is whom we are preaching. We are preaching Jesus Christ as the risen Lord of life. This is not an idea. It has to become very concrete, very real for us. We have to dare to affirm life wherever we see it. Celebrate life, and lift it up.

Lift it up when a little child is born. That is one of the greatest mysteries in the midst of this dark death-oriented world: a little child is being born again and again. We have to celebrate that and see that that's a great event and not sort of a routine event of every day. Two friends are reconciled. You have to dare to see what a great event that is and celebrate it with joy and thanksgiving. We celebrate by the beauty of nature, or are deeply moved by some life-giving art. You have to celebrate it and be aware that that is a sign of the risen Lord. Wherever you go you have to have that diagnostic eye, that careful-looking eye that is willing to recognize life, life happening in between the dark forces of evil, of destruction, darkness, and death.

Keep looking for it. The witness of the living Christ is the one who dares to point to life wherever it takes place. That witness always reveals itself in weakness. It's always small. It's always like a little flower blooming up through the cracks of the concrete. It's always something very precious, very tender, very gentle. You have to look at it and say to each other, "Ah, come here, come here. . . . Oh, you didn't see it? Look carefully. It's beautiful. Come with me, I know someone who loves someone deeply. I want you to meet them. I want you to become a friend of this person who is so full of life that just being with him or her will give you another sense of all that is. Come. Come and see!"

This way resistance doesn't become a heavy, dark job. It becomes a life-giving ray of movement. Somewhere out of that, the "No" will flow easily. Again, the resistance of yes and no really is a form of prayer. I hope that you will see that connection. Resistance is prayer, just as prayer is resistance. Resistance is prayer because it is a proclamation and a confession of the living God.

And why does it take place? First of all, because God is a living God. Period. It is not because it helps, not because you have so many successes, not because it works. That is not the beginning of resistance. You resist in saying Yes and in saying No, simply because you are a human being who wants to proclaim who you are in the presence of God.

There was this little boy who said to the prophet, "Hey, prophet, why are you always talking against those evils in the world? You have been doing that so long and nothing is changing. Why are you doing it?" And the prophet said, "Little boy, I'm not doing it to change the world. I'm doing it to prevent the world from changing me." And that's the core of resistance. We don't protest simply because it works, not simply because it has a lot of success, not simply because now you're on television, or not simply because people are writing about you. That's not the basis of resistance. You resist because it belongs to who you are and who God is. It is the most authentic expression of your humanity. You are life, and you want to speak to that life wherever you are. You resist as an act of authenticity to your own humanity, made in the image of God.

In that sense, it is prayer because it is useless. It doesn't pay out. In that sense. It is liturgy, worship. It is the work of the people of God: *liturgia*. It is very important for you and for me to realize that whatever form of resistance we are involved in, demonstrations or picketing or civil disobedience, they all can be forms of liturgy, of praising God, of giving witness to the living Lord. If you see resistance as prayer, as an act of liturgy in the streets, so to say, or an act of liturgy that is in between the worlds, then you won't be so preoccupied with what the effects of it are. You believe it will be fruitful in its own way and in its own time.

Community

Finally, I want to say something about community. Community is the place of prayer and resistance. Prayer and resistance are not just individual heroic acts. *I* am doing this and *I* am doing that. Prayer and resistance meet in community. The Christian community is the place where peacemaking becomes visible, where the peace itself becomes present. It's not just a medium in order to do certain things better. Community is the reality where we begin seeing what we are after in the first place. Community is a new way of being together and living together in which that peace becomes visible as a light shining in the midst of the darkness.

Community, in whatever form it is, a family, a working group, in local parishes, is a place of ongoing confession and forgiveness. We keep saying again and again to each other, "Listen, I'm weak; I did it again. I was back at that old dark place again. I was acting out of those old hurts again. I was just getting mad as hell because I remembered something of old that just came back to me again." And we have the courage in community to say, "I'm sorry. Can we try again?"

The difference between a Christian community and people loosely scattered in the world is not that only those in a Christian community are sinners and the others are not. Rather, those who are in a Christian community are called to confess to one another their weaknesses, their vulnerability, and continue to lift that up in forgiveness. They give witness to the ongoing love and forgiveness of God who has made peace with us. Without vulnerability, confession, and forgiveness, we grow more and more defensive, distancing ourselves from one another. In that anger and resentment lie the seeds of destruction, war, and annihilation.

Community is that place where we remain vulnerable to each other. In shared vulnerability we make love visible in this world. "Look how they love each other." "Look, how they work together." "Peace is possible, because I've *seen* it."

The community is also the place from which resistance in the world is going to take place. For if community is the birthplace of resistance, it won't take place out of frustration or out of anger. Community provides the space where through prayer and a careful diagnosis of the problems of our day, we feel called to speak up and act together. We don't do it because I have this terrible need to finally get this frustration off my back. We do it because my community, the people of God sent me to be their representative and to act in the name of the Lord. Some may be home praying or doing very simple household tasks. Others might be involved in protest or civil disobedience. Others might be in prison. But all of them, wherever they are as part of that community, are part of peacemaking, because they are part of that community in which the Lord is present and from which they go out.

Let me conclude with this last point that is for me the most important one. Community is to be a eucharistic community. That means a community of thanks-giving. That is the core Christian attitude: gratitude always, in whatever we do, whatever we say, whatever we think. Gratitude is to be the basic disposition. The eucharistic celebration is the core of it, when we lift up the bread and the wine made by human hands to the Lord and the Lord returns those gifts to us, full of his divine acceptance, so that we can be nurtured and strengthened by these gifts. When that mysterious interchange happens, we are in the center of gratitude.

But that gratitude has to be carried out in the world at every moment of our life, so that we always can say, "thank you, thank you" with thankful hearts, aware of God's gifts and God's desire for peace. Life is not a property that we go out to conquer, that we are going to possess, that we are going to defend, that we are going to hold on to at all costs. That is the path that leads to war, conflict, and finally to a holocaust. Life is a gift, a free gift, the abundant gift of God.

And what do we do with that gift? We share it. We give it freely. We give it away. You say, "No, I have only so little, I have only five loaves and a few fishes." Give it away! And it will multiply right under your fingers. Give it away. Don't hold on to it. If you hold on to it, it stays small and it will become smaller and smaller. But if you give it away in the belief that this is God's gift, blessings from him, those little pieces of bread you have and those few fishes you can hold on to will multiply.

Don't hold on to your knowledge, to your affection, to your friends, as if they were properties that are only yours and you are going to keep them. Give them away and you will see there is enough for everybody. Enough food, enough love, enough knowledge, enough affection. Give it away and you will see that it returns to you many times over. That's eucharistic living. That is the life that Jesus speaks about.

So: prayer, resistance, and community. Let us just see those three words again when we read those words of Jesus. "I've told you all these things so that in me you may have peace." In him who dwells in the center of our life. "In this world you will have trouble." But in this world we say No to death and Yes to life and thus relate to that trouble from a place of peace. "But take heart. I have overcome the world." Everything has already been accomplished in him and we, wherever we go, and whatever we do, and whomever we meet, we are announcing gratefully the gift of God that has already been given to us. Amen.

The Broken World, the Broken Self, and Community

In this address to the Catholic Youth Corps at Convocation Hall in Toronto in April 1987, Henri describes what he has been learning about human brokenness, loneliness, and community since following the call he received to join L'Arche Daybreak in August 1986.

We live in a broken world. You have seen broken bodies, broken by hunger, broken by sickness, broken by physical and mental abuse. And you've seen broken faces, broken by guilt and shame and depression. And you have heard voices, the voice of a world full of anguish. Out of all that that you have seen and heard there is this prayer coming forth: "Swing low, sweet chariot. Swing low, sweet mercy. Swing low, sweet compassion. Swing low, sweet Jesus." I've been thinking about all of that, and wondering what it means. What I start seeing is that Christ is being crucified again.

In our world today, Jesus is truly nailed against the blue globe of God's creation. We see in suffering humanity that Jesus is nailed to our world, and he is crying out, "My God, my God, why have you abandoned me?" And you know, the question is not, for me at least, "Why, O God, do you allow all this pain to exist?" For me, the question has become, "Why did you swing so low to become part of us, to enter into all of this? Why, sweet Jesus, did you swing so low and suffer it all with us?" And there is an answer. The answer I am gradually hearing is, "I swing low, dear brother, I swing low, dear sister, to lead you out of the house of fear into the house of love. I don't want you to be so afraid. I want you to love."

Have you ever noticed how afraid we all are? We are afraid of what is happening right in our own inner selves: the tensions, the impulses, the anguish, the loneliness. We are afraid of the strangers around us. They frighten us.

What I want you to know, first of all, is that it is fear inside us that creates so much of the anguish we see in our broken world. What is that fear really about? It is fear of death. We are so afraid to die. So many things that remind us of death, sickness and illness, war and torture, and poverty around us, make us afraid and we withdraw. And the more afraid we are, the more we start harming ourselves.

You know quite well that the agenda of this world is the agenda of fear. But Jesus says something totally different. He says, "Do not be afraid." Those same words recur throughout the gospels. It is what the angel says to Zechariah, and what the angel says to Mary. It is what Jesus says to the women at the tomb, and to his disciples at the lake. "Do not be afraid. It is I. Have no fear." All over the gospels you hear that voice: "Brothers, sisters, do not be afraid, it is I." You don't have to live in the house of fear.

Let me ask you something. Can you hear that voice that says, "Do not be afraid?" Can you hear it?

How do we move out of this house of fear? Is there an answer? I think we hear an answer from the evangelist John, where he writes about love. He says: "Let us love one another, because God has loved us first." John does not say, "Let us love one another so we can solve each other's problems, so that we can feel good about each other." No, John says, "Let us love one another, because we have been loved first by God." It is precisely this first love that enables us to let go of our fear: You are loved. You are accepted, long before you could receive or give love. That is the great news of the gospel. You are fully, totally loved.

You are not what other people say you are. You are not what other people think about you or do to you. You are not the opinions of others or the affection of others or the rejection of others. That's not who you are. That's not who we are. You are who God made you to be. You are the fruit of God's love, that first love.

Solitude

How do we become part of God's first love? I have a simple word for you, and I want you to hear it well. The place where you can hear the voice of the first love is called solitude. Solitude is where you can listen and where you can hear a voice that says: "Do not be afraid. I love you." That voice says: "I have loved you long before anyone loved you." And you have to dare to enter into that solitude so that your aloneness does not become loneliness. In solitude you can enter into the presence of God and let God speak in the center of your heart and tell you what you so much want to hear: "You are loved. You are completely loved."

As long as you run around all over the world, looking for

affection, you cannot hear that voice. You remain deaf. The Latin word for deaf is *surdus*. If you are very, very deaf, you are *absurdus*. An absurd life is precisely a life in which you no longer hear that voice that says, "I love you." So we keep on running around asking that question, "Do you love me? I'm so afraid you don't."

But when you dare to enter into solitude, you can listen. And the Latin word for listening is *audire* and to listen with great attention is *ob-audire*. Solitude means a life of obedience, listening to the voice of love. So let us be quiet. You do not have to be lonely anymore. Turn your loneliness into solitude. From that place of solitude in your heart you can gradually grow the vision of hope. You can do this, because it is in solitude that you are able to hear that loving voice that will give you hope.

Community

It is not very easy to stay in solitude. In our solitude we hear so many voices and not only the voice of love. You hear voices that say, "Do this," or "Go there." "You forgot this. You forgot that." Sometimes in our solitude, we are so overwhelmed by those voices.

But if we dare to stay and persevere in our solitude, we will gradually hear more and more that voice of love underneath all our restlessness. As we listen to that voice that says to us, "I love you," we discover that it is the same voice, saying the same thing to all people.

In solitude, we discover a space that is so wide that there is enough room for everyone. Solitude becomes the place from which we can go to our friends and our brothers and sisters and greet them. Not out of loneliness, but out of solitude.

We can start forming community, because community

means solitude greeting solitude. My solitude, in which I have discovered how much I am loved, greets your solitude in which you have discovered how much you are loved. When we come together as solitude greeting solitude, we form a new home, a new house. No longer are we living in the house of fear, but in the house of love. In that house, there is space to welcome others. There is space for the stranger to walk in and feel welcome. There is space for the poor and the broken to receive hospitality.

I want to talk to you about that community that grows out of solitude, because that is where our hope can grow stronger and deeper. I have just recently joined a community, the community of L'Arche Daybreak, close to Toronto in Richmond Hill. I really don't know too much about community because for twenty years I was teaching and sort of hugging my loneliness and holding on to my separation. So, I am a newcomer to community, but I'm gradually learning. I would like to say a few things about that, because I feel that community is where hope can grow in the midst of this world.

Community is, first of all, the place of intimacy. If you are afraid, you cannot be intimate. You cannot be intimate with a person you're afraid of. If you are afraid of a person you either cling to them or you run away. Real intimacy is something other than clinging or running. It means the willingness to truly be together in weakness and to be faithful to one another in our vulnerability.

There was a time that I talked a lot about love and friendship, but then I went home and I did what I wanted to do and lived how I wanted to live and nobody could check me out. Now I live in community, and, oh my dear, they know everything about me. They check me out every second, not out of suspicion, but basically saying, "Hey Henri, what you just said, what you spoke about, are you living it out too?"

Gradually I am discovering that community is the place of intimacy, because it's the place where we have to continue to confess to each other that we aren't able to live up to all our ideals. In community you have to forgive each other continuously. But the beauty of community, of friendship, of marriage, and the beauty of living together is that every time we say, "I'm sorry, brother, I'm sorry, sister. I'm sorry that I am not the way that you want me to be," we can hear the other person say, "That's all right. I love you," and then the intimacy grows deeper and stronger. So I'm learning that community is the place of ongoing confession and ongoing forgiveness.

Growing closer to each other in this ongoing confession and forgiveness, we discover that God, the one who truly loves us, is greater than we are. We come in touch with God's first love through confession and forgiveness in community. We experience that we are held together in community by a God who is faithful to us.

Community is also the place of fruitfulness. That's a beautiful word that I want you to take home. It's a word that is very important in community. We can bear fruit. Our society is not very interested in fruit. Our society is interested in products. Our society is interested in you and I making things that we can sell. We want to be productive people who make a lot of things. I do this, I do that, and if I do that enough I am very productive.

Community is a place where we bear fruit in weakness, where we come together as broken people. But that brokenness can bear fruit. In my community at Daybreak they are plowing the ground to start the garden. I learned that the ground has to be broken open so that it can bear fruit. It has to be weak. It has to be soft. It has to be crumbling. Then something can grow. If it is hard, if it is stiff, new growth won't come. And that is what community is about. We become broken soil for each other, in which new life can come forth. That is the beauty of intimacy. Two people come together in total vulnerability without anything to protect them. Then new life can be born. That life is a fruit of their love.

We have to remain aware that in community we meet in weakness. We are invited to be vulnerable, real. When we come together as broken people, you are very weak. When I came to Daybreak, they asked me to take care of a young man called Adam. Adam cannot speak or walk. Adam cannot dress or undress himself. He needs help every step of the way of his life. He is twenty-five years old, but totally dependent. Adam needs my help. And I see his weakness.

I carry him to his bath in the morning. I take Adam to his breakfast. It takes a long time to do it all. But the more I have come to know Adam, the more I have realized how fruitful his life is. He calls me and us to solitude. And at the same time he creates a community around him that is caring. Around his weak, broken person, people stand and come together from different countries, with different personalities, with different characters, but they form community around Adam who knows them. When I am with him in silence, I realize how Adam says to me, without saying anything, "Henri, quiet down, take it easy, slow down, and trust that things are all right." He doesn't have to say a word to let me know that.

Community is also the place of joy and celebration. That's what I am learning. In community, people take a long time to eat together. And I think: "Let's get this over so I can get to work." But eating is celebration, being together. We take our time for it. When there is a sad moment, we celebrate. When there is a happy moment, we celebrate. When somebody has a birthday, we celebrate. When somebody comes, we celebrate;

when somebody leaves, we celebrate. When somebody feels sad, we talk about it. When somebody feels happy, we lift it up, because celebration is lifting up the moment and saying: "God is here. Now. This is the day the Lord has made. This is the moment we want to acclaim and proclaim as a moment of togetherness with God."

Celebration means the awareness that God is a God of the present moment. You do not have to cling to the guilt of the past, nor reach out in fear of the future. We can truly say, what is happening is happening here and now. And we want to lift it up as a source of joy. Community is the place where we can say, "Here and now something is happening that is good, even when it hurts. Even when it is painful, even when it creates anguish in us. Let's not run away from it." Just as Jesus was saying to those people on the road to Emmaus, "You people, didn't you know that the Son of Man had to suffer and so enter into his glory?" Suddenly we realize that in the painful moments, there's a little glory hidden. You have to lift that up and bring it out.

No, that is not easy. Because we always think that the real thing is going to happen tomorrow, or next week or next year, or when we leave school or when we get a new job or later in life. But the truth is, all we need is always here.

So community, dear friends, is the place of intimacy, the place of fruitfulness, the place of celebration. I want to say that for you, and for all of us, that is the place where the vision of hope is being born. You do not live in the same type of community that I do. But you are being called, just as I am, to form community, whether it is in your parish, your family, among friends—wherever we are being called to live our life as Christians. This life is one in which we dare to enter into solitude and discover how much we are loved. We can rise from that solitude and form communities in which we can truly celebrate life and be a sign of hope in this world.

Let me conclude with a text that I read in the Gospel of Luke. It is a very beautiful text where Jesus speaks about the end times. He says, nations will fight nations. People will fight people. There will be anguish and there'll be war. People will run away out of fear. "Oh, but you, my friends," says Jesus, "pray unceasingly to survive what is going to happen, so that you can hold ground confidently in the presence of the Son of Man. Hear this well."

Pray unceasingly to survive what is going to happen and hold your ground confidently in the presence of the Son of Man. That's really what we talked about today. The call to solitude is to pray unceasingly, and it is a call to hold ground together as a community. In the midst of this world, there will be more wars and more conflicts. The anguish and the pain of this world will not just vanish. But we do not have to be destroyed by it. We can live together in solitude and community, praying unceasingly and holding ground together.

We can stand confidently with our heads held high gazing on the Son of Man to sustain us together. Then we can do away with all the compulsions of our culture—money, self-righteousness, conflict, and dogmatism. We can say: You don't need all that. You don't need all this holding on to human-made truth. We can have hope. For we have received a new heart, no longer a bitter heart or heart of stone, but a heart of flesh.

Holding Ground

Following a trip to visit a L'Arche community in Honduras, Henri was moved to explore what the North American church could learn from Christian communities in Central America about faithfulness and solidarity in the face of long-standing systemic injustice. His reflections explored many aspects of the history and the current political violence in Central America. The excerpts here focus on the implications of community. The full essay was published in the publication CALC Report *by Baltimore Clergy and Laity Concerned (CALC) in 1987.*

A few months ago I made a short trip to Honduras. In contrast to previous visits to Central America, I didn't go to get better informed about the nature of the conflict that keeps the region in turmoil and the role of the United States. I simply went there to make a retreat with people of L'Arche, a network of communities for mentally handicapped people. I didn't visit any politicians, nor any church leaders. The only thing I was able to do was to spend some hours in the small L'Arche community in Suyapa close to Tegucigalpa.

There I met Raphael. Raphael is a deeply handicapped young man, unable to walk, speak, dress, or feed himself. He has black hair, dark brown skin, and a beautiful, almost translucent face. Seven years ago he was found in a mental institution in Tegucigalpa and brought to Casa Nazareth to be the first member of El Arca de Honduras. As I sat with Raphael and tried to communicate with him, I wondered what this silent and completely dependent, handicapped young man was telling me about the Central American conflict and the Christian response to it. . . .

A few years ago I responded to the explosive situation in the Central American region by lobbying in the U.S. Congress and calling on the churches to say "No" to starting a second Vietnam below our southern borders. Now I was sitting with Raphael, wondering what kind of response he and his family of handicapped people were calling for. As I sat there holding his hand, words that I had often heard, but never fully understood, started to re-emerge in my mind:

> "When you hear of wars and revolutions, do not be terrified, for this is something that must happen first, but the end will not come at once. . . . And then they will see the Son of Man coming in a cloud with power and great glory. When these things begin to take place, stand erect, hold your heads high because your liberation is near at hand. . . . Stay awake, praying at all times for the strength to survive all that is going to happen, and to hold your ground before the Son of Man." (Luke 21:9–36)

As I squeezed Raphael's hand and felt his powerlessness and dependency, these words of Jesus received a new meaning for me. "Hold your ground before the Son of Man." It seemed that Raphael was telling me in his utter weakness not to let the powers and principalities surrounding me seduce me to fear and panic, but to hold my spiritual ground and stand confidently in the presence of the Lord, knowing that liberation is near at hand. He didn't tell me that I should not lobby or make speeches; he didn't tell me that I shouldn't protest against violence; he didn't tell me that I shouldn't act courageously to unmask the powers of evil; but his broken crucified body warned me never to surrender to fear, to pray unceasingly, and to act faithfully by waiting for the Lord who is coming to judge the living and the dead.

So I will speak in Raphael's name about "holding ground." It is the ground of prayer and action.

Prayer

"Pray at all times for the strength to survive all that is going to happen." These words remind us that we have first of all to survive spiritually in the midst of the noise, the bewilderment, and the agony that surround us. Fear, anger, frustration, impatience, resentment, revenge, and hatred for the enemy are only a few of the temptations that can easily make us lose ground and be destroyed by the cares of life. The call to pray at all times is a call to live a life intimately connected with the suffering Christ.

But unless we keep our eyes fixed on Jesus, the suffering we see will consume us.

To pray means to keep our hearts always united with the heart of Jesus and thus, in and through this union, see and hear the cry of the poor, not to arouse our passion but to awaken true compassion.

This deeply pervasive state of servitude can give us a glimpse of the living Christ who entered into solidarity with the poor. In the oppressed, manipulated, and tortured people of Central

America the suffering Christ reveals himself to us. He entered with his people in servitude, carries their burdens with them, and offers his life for them in the struggle for liberation.

I consider it a question of spiritual survival to recognize the descending Christ wherever we see a victimized people. Through this recognition we come in touch with the mind of the one who didn't cling to his divine place of power, but emptied himself of all power and took on the status of a slave. Is it possible for us to look at this humiliated Christ in the face, to feel compassion for this Christ, and to start binding up his many wounds? Only if we are willing to follow the same descending road that Jesus followed and move from competition to compassion, from rivalry to forgiveness, from power to a powerlessness, from individualism to community. Seeing Christ in the poor of Central America is only possible when that same Christ has found a place in our own heart. And the only place in our heart where Christ can dwell is the place of weakness, the place where we can connect ourselves with Christ's descending way. That is very, very hard in an upwardly mobile society ruled by ambition and power. But we will never truly be able to hold our ground before the Son of Man if we use our competitive selves to show compassion, and our arrogance to nurture the humble.

Thus the oppressed and dependent people of Central America represent the living Christ calling us to take up our own cross before we take up theirs and follow Him to the place of utter abandonment. When I say that prayer is the first and most important Christian response to the suffering of the Central American people, I do not mean simply that we ought to pray for those who are so obviously worse off than we are. No, by prayer I mean connecting our own weak vulnerable heart with the suffering heart of Jesus and thus living a life with the mind of Christ; by prayer I mean to claim our anguish, fear, guilt,

and anger and to take them up as our own true cross and thus
to begin to experience solidarity with the suffering Christ in
Central America. By prayer I mean to walk in the same humble
way of Christ which the poor of Central America are walking
and thus experience in our innermost being the truth that our
common immersion in the cleansing water of Christ binds us
together in ways far transcending national, cultural, economic,
or ethnic bonds.

As long as we keep clinging to our false identity as the spiritual powerbrokers of the world who are quite willing to help
the poor and oppressed of Central America, and offer them our
Christian service, we are not much different from the political and economic powerbrokers who caused the suffering we
are trying to relieve. Only when we are willing to build a new
fellowship, a fellowship of the weak, first among ourselves and
then with our brothers and sisters in Central America, only then
can we trust that it will be possible to survive what is going to
happen and to hold ground before the Son of Man.

When I held the hands of Raphael in Suyapa and let his utter weakness speak to me, I didn't hear: "Do this, or do that for
my people," but I heard: "Let Jesus touch you where you are as
weak as I am, so that we both can belong to him." He called
me away from the world that wants to solve all problems and
invited me to join him on the hard and liberating way of the
cross. He reminded me that I do not belong to the world any
more than Jesus belongs to the world and made me aware that
unceasing prayer was the only sure way not to become victimized by the powers of the world and lose my ground before the
Son of Man. It is very hard to hear this. So much in me wants
to solve problems, change structures, alter the course of history,
and claim victory over the power of evil. The way of Raphael is

the least likely way for me to choose. But it is God's way and therefore the only way to true liberation.

Action

"Stay awake and hold your ground." These words are not only a call to prayer but also a call to action. This becomes very clear when Jesus describes in more detail the day on which the Son of Man is coming in judgment. On that day all nations will be assembled before him and he will raise the question: "What have you done for the least of mine?" "Doing" is important; it is even the final criterion by which we will be judged.

When we look critically at the long history of oppression and manipulation in Central America it is not so simple to answer the question what "doing something for the poor in Central America" means. Many actions seemed like steps into a vast morass. Countless people have given a lot of money, time, and energy to respond to the nutritional, medical, and educational needs of the poor in Central America; many have witnessed courageously for peace and reconciliation, and quite a few have dedicated their lives to the Central American struggle for liberation. But it is hard to claim much success. The overall picture of dependency and poverty has not changed; the old patterns of exploitation have basically remained the same; and violence and the threat of war seem to be as visible now as they were when our consciences were first awakened.

It is hardly likely that the future will see a radical change in the official U.S. attitude towards its southern neighbors. It is not realistic to expect that the patterns of direct interference into the political and economic affairs of the Central American countries will drastically change, that human rights violations and military interventions will significantly decrease, and that the poor will live much better during the coming decades. The signs which Jesus mentions—nation fighting against nation, famines in various places, persecutions and imprisonment, people fainting away with terror and fear—will continue to be present to warn us not to be seduced by them and to remain faithful in the midst of it all.

So, what then does action mean for a Christian surrounded by these calamities? Let me try to articulate some directions.

Action must be born out of love. Every action, even the most generous, when born out of fear, anger, guilt, or frustration, cannot bear fruit. It might draw much attention, stir up many feelings, motivate many people, but it will not find a fertile ground where it can give new life. The place from which Christian action comes forth is the place beyond the structures of the world. It is the place where we truly belong. It is the place of forgiveness, reconciliation, community, and compassion. In short, it is the place where we can love our friends as well as our enemies.

Maybe the love of our enemy is the best criterion by which to evaluate the authenticity of a Christian action, because when we are able to truly love our enemy, whether it is an enemy in the U.S. or Central America, we have a clear sign that we belong to God "who causes the sun to rise on the bad as well as the good and sends down rain to fall on the upright and the wicked alike" (Matt. 5:45). Belonging to the world means dividing the world into those who are for you and those who are against you. Belonging to God means seeing the world as a world whose people are all deeply and intimately loved and thus are truly brothers and sisters. Whatever we do, therefore, should be done with the universal compassion of God. From that place we are sent into the world to act, not in reaction to what the world does, but in response to who God is.

Action must have the quality of receiving. If, indeed, the suffering Christ can be discerned among the people of Central America, a Christ who calls us to conversion, then we have to be willing to receive the gifts of the suffering Christ from the people. This is a very central aspect of action. It is setting the poor free to offer their gifts. After centuries in which the poor of Central America have been made to believe that they have only to receive—culture, economic aid, and true religion— and nothing to offer, the most urgent action is to reverse this oppressive process and discover with the poor their own spiritual wealth. Those who have lived for any length of time among the people of Central America in the Spirit of Jesus will readily acknowledge that they have received more than they could ever give. Often they became deeply aware of their own spiritual poverty when they saw the rich spiritual gifts that the poor offered them: "love, joy, peace, patience, kindness, goodness, faithfulness, gentleness, and self-control" (Gal. 5:22). They came to realize that amidst tremendous suffering Jesus had touched the poor so deeply that they became true messengers of good news.

A stay among the Christians of Central America can make us realize how our own fast and competitive society has become pervaded with fear, sorrow, violence, impatience, revenge, malice, lies, and licentiousness, and open our eyes to the fact that even in our own Christian communities the Spirit of Christ has often been extinguished and replaced by the spirit of the world.

It was only after a long stay among the poor down South that I started to see how somber, serious, and guilt-ridden my fellow Christians up North were. I had taken their collective depression for granted until I saw the exuberant joy and the free expression of love and affection among those who in their poverty still are deeply aware of God's preferential love.

If any action is necessary, it is to free the people of South and Central America from their fatalism, self-rejection, and low self-esteem and help them claim the rich spiritual fruits of their suffering as a gift to lift up, celebrate, and share. The beauty of receiving such gifts is that the givers discover that they have something to offer. A gift becomes a real gift through the grateful eyes of the receiver. One of the tasks that is ours is to find always new and creative ways in which this receiving, and thus revealing, of gifts can take place. Thus we participate in the great and joyful work of human liberation.

Action must have a communal quality. Action in solidarity with the people of Central America must not simply be perceived as action that comes from the initiatives of concerned Christians, but as the action of the whole Christian community. By making our action an action by the living body of Christ, through the community of those whose lives are being incorporated into the life of the crucified and risen Lord, our action becomes indeed a way of holding our ground in the presence of the Son of Man. We lose ground the moment we allow the world to perceive our action as an expression of a splinter group from the left or right and not of the whole body.

The Church must act as Church, offering support, encouragement, and comfort to those parts of the body that need special care. This requires much patience and hard work, but in the long run the rewards will be evident.

These are only a few aspects of the active side of holding our ground in the presence of the Son of Man. By making our action prayerful, grateful, and communal it can indeed become an authentic Christian response to the Central American reality. Thus our actions won't be dependent on success, but can be judged by their fruits. They won't be motivated by hope of influence, but by authenticity, and won't be judged by their impact, but by their intention. If we as Christians are worried about the number of people involved, the amount of TV and newspaper coverage achieved, and the obvious results, we are driving in the fast lane leading to disillusionment, burn-out, and self-destruction.

The way to liberation of the people of Central America is a very slow way. The sins of five centuries are not undone in one generation. For the Christian community the question is not whether what we do "works," but whether it is a faithful response to the crisis as seen by the eyes of faith. Jesus was a failure in the eyes of the world and so were his followers St. Paul, St. Francis, and Dorothy Day. They had nothing to brag about when they died. Their work was small, insignificant, and easily discarded as useless. But they are the salt of the earth and the light of the world. What offers us hope is not that they solved the problems of their time, but that they responded to them in faithfulness to their vocation as Christians. The question for us on the Day of Judgment will not be: "Did you solve the problems of Central America?" but "Did you respond to them in the Spirit of Jesus?"

St. Francis didn't solve any problems of his time, but his faithful response to them continues to be a source of hope many centuries after his death. Indeed, his actions were not successful, but very fruitful. And so were the actions of Oscar Romero, Rutilio Grande, the four church women in El Salvador, and many other unnamed Christians who gave their lives in the struggle for justice and peace. Our actions are called to be the same. What is important is whether we as individuals and communities are holding our ground in the presence of the Son of Man.

The small community in Suyapa surrounding Raphael is very fragile. A handful of mentally handicapped persons, a handful of assistants from Honduras, France, Belgium, Brazil, and the U.S., the loving support of a few families in Tegucigalpa, and many kids walking in and out of the house. There are many smiles, long hours sitting around the table just talking, and frequent prayers. There are always visitors.

During the hours I spent there I was struck by the power of the powerless. Compared with all the noises about U.S. military bases and Contra aid and the threat of war, this little community looked like a little rose petal on a stormy ocean. But sitting around the table and seeing the joy and peace on the faces of Raphael and his new family, I felt the power of love as I seldom feel it. I asked myself: Is it the fragile, unknown communities like this that keep the world from being blown up? Is it the gentle joy and peace of the poor that makes our loving Lord show his mercy again towards a sinful generation? Is it the Raphaels of this world in whose brokenness the compassionate Father recognizes his Son crucified for the salvation of humanity?

As I saw this small community hidden away in a world quickly running toward the edge of the abyss, I felt a real hope emerging in me. I had been wondering for so many years what to do about the situation in Central America and after much lobbying and speaking, trying to convince the powers of the world to change its course, this little community appeared to me as the group of women who took the body of Jesus from the cross, accompanied it to the grave, and kept watch there. It is an action that seems so useless and so completely futile. But binding the wounds of the broken body of Jesus, covering it with a shroud and laying it in the sepulcher, and waiting there, isn't that the greatest act of faith? Are we supposed to save the world? Are we going to resurrect the dead, make peace, and establish the kingdom? No, we are not. And if we are trying to take over God's work we will destroy ourselves.

Maybe, maybe caring for the broken body of Raphael and gently stroking his silent face and carrying him into his bed and praying him to sleep, maybe that is a way of preparing ourselves to recognize the risen Lord when he will appear to us on Easter morning. The world will continue to fight, oppress, kill, and destroy, but happy are those who can hear his voice and see his face as he walks with us on the road.

Prayer, Community, and Action

By speaking about prayer and action in response to the Central American reality, I have tried to restate concretely the Christian call to be in the world without belonging to it, to work for peace and justice while never losing touch with the One in whom we find our identity, to say "No" to the power of death while staying truly alive, to act courageously while praying confidently.

Unceasing prayer and loving, grateful, communal action are the ways to hold our ground while the world tries to seduce us to hatred, violence, and war. By way of conclusion I will try to make some concrete suggestions based on the reflections I have presented to you. I hope I speak in the name of Raphael and many other little people of Central America.

Keep your eyes fixed on the suffering Jesus. "Come to me," he says, "all you who labor and are overburdened and I will give you rest. Learn from me, for I am gentle and humble of heart." As long as we keep our eyes fixed on the agony of humanity outside of the heart of Jesus we will be reduced to depression or anger and become the victim of the demons we are fighting.

To keep our eyes fixed on the suffering Jesus we have to dare to spend long hours in solitude. There at the heart of Jesus from which blood and water flow, our own anxious heart and the heart of a world in agony can become one in the womb of God and there we can find the peace and the joy the world cannot give.

The stronger we feel the need for resistance, protests, and relief work, the more we must balance out these actions with solitude where we can be with God and God alone. Without such solitude our actions cannot remain an expression of faith, but will quickly degenerate into an erratic attempt to overcome a demonically inspired fatalism.

When we want to take seriously the call to pray without ceasing, we need to withdraw in a quiet place often and there listen to the One who wants to cast out our fear with his perfect love and show us how to carry that love into our world as a light into the darkness.

Form communities of love. A community of love is a community in which God's perfect love is made visible by an ongoing mutual confession and forgiveness. The Christian people of Central America call us to discover what it means to be Church. More important than anything we say or do for the people in Central America is allowing them to help us rediscover the beauty of living as a community of faith. The success-oriented world in which we live has co-opted the Christian community in many ways. This is the time to reclaim, with the help of our suffering neighbors, our identity as a fellowship of the weak, held together by Our Lord. It is in such communities that we can find the safe space to let go of our illusions of grandeur, strip ourselves of our desire for power and influence, and discover our own vulnerable self where Jesus has chosen to dwell.

The great challenge of the people of Central America to us is to discover our identity as Church, people of God, the living body of Christ.

Discern your unique call to action. When our hearts are fixed on Jesus through a discipline of solitude and when we have grown into a true fellowship of the weak through the discipline of community, we can faithfully discern our special responsibility as individuals and communities towards the Central American people.

We are not called to heroism, but to martyrdom. Heroism calls attention to ourselves. Martyrdom calls attention to God. Martyrs are witnesses who give all they have, yes, even their lives, to manifest the love of God. What then is our unique form of witness? In which way are we called to action? Giving money? Lobbying in Congress? Calling the Church to a deeper solidarity with the suffering people in Central America? Witnessing for peace at the Nicaraguan borders? Visiting political and ecclesiastical leaders in El Salvador, Guatemala, Honduras, Nicaragua, Costa Rica, and Panama? Starting clinics, language schools, or orphanages? Working for and with the refugees in the sanctuary movement or otherwise? Adopting a child of parents killed in the violence? Writing letters, participating in nonviolent resistance? Going to prison for acts of civil disobedience?

Yes, all of that, some of that, or none of that, depending on whether it is truly discerned as a faith response to the reality we live. Once we have come to know in our solitude how God calls us and have been affirmed by the community, then we can truly act no longer in our own name, but in the Name of Christ and act with hope, courage, and confidence.

Acting in the name of Christ always means acting in the name of his Body, the Church, because Christ and his Church can never be separated. It is this deep connection with Christ and his Church that makes even our smallest action part of the great divine work of liberation. Once we know that what we do is truly part of the greater work of God and God's people, we can do it with our whole being. Then all we do will bear fruit, whether it is giving a cup of cold water to a child or laying down one's life for one's friend, because all is part of the unbreakable network of faith. So let us keep our eyes fixed on Jesus, form communities of faith, and discern our own unique call to action. Only thus will we be able to survive all that is going to happen and hold our ground before the Son of Man. May Raphael and all the poor of Central America be our guides.

From Communion to Community

The Contemplative Journey

Henri delivered this lecture at Regis College, University of Toronto, on February 27, 1991. In this previously unpublished presentation, he describes how moving from Harvard to L'Arche Daybreak deepened his understanding and his practice of community as an expression of communion with God.

> *Now during those days he went out to the mountain to pray; and he spent the night in prayer to God. And when day came, he called his disciples and chose twelve of them, whom he also named apostles: Simon, whom he named Peter, and his brother Andrew, and James, and John, and*

*Philip, and Bartholomew, and Matthew,
and Thomas, and James son of Alphaeus,
and Simon, who was called the Zealot, and
Judas son of James, and Judas Iscariot, who
became a traitor.*

—LUKE 6:12–16

In coming to L'Arche from Harvard and the academic world, I was coming out of a very individualistic world that says "try to do it by yourself." So I went out and tried to do a lot of things. And finally, I realized that wasn't working and maybe I should choose community. And I came to L'Arche Daybreak, and they said, "Well, Henri, are you praying?"

So my life is gradually rediscovering the right order of things. I might have come to that order through the back door. But I have begun to realize that we are called to a life of communion and to let community grow out of that communion. And to minister really means to call people to communion. I want to speak about those three words—communion, community, and ministry—and then to share some of what I have learned from my own life in community.

All three parts of this movement from communion to community to ministry are very beautiful and very painful. The passage from Luke, chapter 6, describes Jesus in communion with God in the night, then his act of forming community with his disciples, including one of them who became a traitor. This community led him to ministry, and it was his ministry among people that led Jesus to the cross.

So communion, community, and ministry are places where we want to be, but also where we experience great pain and great struggle. I think that you and I are people who cry out for communion and long to discover it.

The Search for Belonging

We want to be people who know what it is to belong somewhere. There is somewhere where I am "home." There is a place where I am well-held, well-embraced, and well-loved. If I think about the people I meet in my own community, but also in my life in the city and in this world, I see people as human beings screaming out for communion, crying out for a place of safety, for a safe place of unity. I think that all of us in very different ways, maybe, are people who are so aware of our brokenness and of the broken connections in our life. There is a constant hunger for communion, for healing, for restoration, for being united again, and for returning to that place where our hearts can rest and be at peace.

God has created us with a heart that yearns for communion. Much of what we do during the day and during the night is an attempt to achieve that communion. Quite often it's in that search for restoring the connection that we often find ourselves being wounded, being hurt and broken again. Our flesh yearns for intimacy, for the place of rest. Our minds search for an understanding that brings things together. Beyond all of that there is a spirit in us that yearns. And I hope that you are willing to listen to that yearning heart when I speak about communion. Jesus is the one who came to offer us this communion. If we want to have an understanding of what communion means, you have to look at him first. So look at Jesus for a moment. He spent the night in communion with God.

I want you to look at Jesus in the night because it's from that place of communion that we can understand the ministry and the presence of Jesus. When you think about Jesus, think about him as the one who heard the voice that said to him, "You are my beloved. On you my favor rests." That's the voice that he heard when he came out of the Jordan, after his baptism. And Jesus is the one who knows that it is as the Beloved of God, as the one who lives in communion with God, that he is sent into the world.

To believe in Jesus is to believe that in him, you are touching the one with whom he lived in communion. It's very clear in the gospel that when he says, "Do you believe?" he is really saying, "Do you trust?" When you see me or you touch me and you hear me, you hear the one who has sent me, the one with whom I live in communion. The words I'm speaking, Jesus says, I am not speaking for myself. The Father gave me these words to speak to you. The works that I am doing are not my own works. The Father sends me to do these works. The glory I'm receiving is the glory of the Father.

"Do you believe and do you trust that I am the one who lives in full communion with the one who sent me? That's the source and that is the place from which I speak, from which I act, from which I work." Jesus has entered into the night, and he goes to the mountaintop and prays there. Praying means listening to the voice that says, "You are my Beloved. You are my favored one with whom I live in ongoing, unceasing communion. You are the one in whom all my love becomes visible. It is the love with which I have created the universe. That love becomes flesh. I spoke the world through you out of love. And now I send you into the world as the one who is the full expression of my love. The fullness of my love can be touched, seen, and heard." And when Jesus goes to the mountaintop, he goes to the place where he listens to that voice that calls him "the Beloved."

Listening as Obedience

Jesus is the one who listened. Listening comes from the Latin word *audire*. And to listen with great attention is *ob-audire*, obedience. Jesus is the obedient one who listens to the voice that says, "You are my Beloved."

And this is what I invite you to realize: That this is precisely what Jesus wants you and me to be, the beloved sons and daughters of God. When Jesus says it's good for you that I go so I can send you my spirit, he is saying it is good for me to go so I can send you my communion, so that the communion within which I live can be yours. This is true, because you are no less a child of God than I am a child of God. I have come to bring you that communion. And it is from that communion that I want to send you into the world.

And therefore to pray at the mountaintop, to spend the night in prayer, is to continually hear the voice that calls you the Beloved. And it is only as the Beloved of God, as the beloved daughter, as the beloved son of God, that you might start to get an inkling of what it means to live in community and to minister. I say this with an understanding that we are doing many, many things. But quite often, what we do, and what we sometimes call ministry, is done in a way that prevents or avoids the very communion we most desire.

But if you want to know the meaning of Jesus' healing and preaching and teaching, return to that place where he is in communion with God early in the morning, long before dawn. He went to a lonely place and prayed there. And then the disciples came and said, "Everybody's waiting for you." And he says, "Yes, we have to go and we have to preach and we have to announce, but what I am announcing, what I am proclaiming, and from where the power of healing comes is precisely from that place of communion."

The Pain of Communion

But when I say that, I have to say something else too. Communion was lived in the night. Sometimes we think about communion as something very satisfying, that fulfills the needs of my heart and my mind. But I want you to realize that Jesus entered into communion with God during the night. Communion does not necessarily come to you immediately or all at once. In fact, the longer you pray, the more you will be aware that the communion that is given to you and that you are called to live is a communion beyond the feelings of your little heart and the thoughts of your little mind. You are in communion with One who is larger than our minds and hearts.

And that's why you live in communion. It's not something that is easily realized. It requires a very hard discipline. My little heart that yearns for communion is impatient and wants to get something going to make me feel better. When I am yearning for communion, when I'm screaming for a sense of togetherness, I may do two things: I may find myself going to a place that makes me feel well or to a person with whom I can feel well. These are both ways of avoiding the night, the place where real communion is being lived. And you know quite well how hard that is.

The Spirit of God dwells in the deepest places of your heart, in the center of your being; it is there that the spirit of communion is given to you. But the voices of the world around you are calling you all over the place: Go here, there, do this, do that. If you listen to those voices you are always distracted, you're always invited to dissipate yourself, to go to a foreign country, to walk away from home. And the farther you walk away from home, you always end up, like the Prodigal Son, living with the pigs.

You want to find communion, but you go further and further away from home. Staying home or living at home is very hard. Much of that happens in the darkness, in the night. But that's where Jesus comes from. And he says, I want you to be where I am. Neither you nor I belong to the world. You belong to God, you belong to my home. You belong to communion, and from that communion I'm sending you into the world. And so for a moment, try to think about yourself as belonging to the home of God, to the family of God, to the communion of God. And from that place where all is one, you are sent into the world to form community and to minister.

That's a reversal of our usual thinking. That's theological thinking. The word "theology" originally meant "union with God." *Theologia*, that word in its original sense, meant the third level of mystical prayer, communion with God. And I want to tell you that from that place, to the degree that you are entering into that communion, you cannot do other than create community and ministry. It flows from there. Everything Jesus says and does comes from that communion. We hear his words: "You all believe me, that my Father will never leave me alone. I belong to the Father and the Father belongs to me." And later we hear him say: "My God, my God, why have you abandoned me?" But it's a prayer to the One to whom Jesus listens. Communion in total darkness. We hear his final words from the cross: "Into your hands I commend my spirit." It's that communion that Jesus dies to give us. That is the communion that finally, when Jesus is gone, becomes the source of life in the Spirit given to us by God.

I have an icon with me, Rublev's icon of the Trinity. When there was a big war in Russia in the 14th century, all the monks in a big monastery outside of Moscow were very anxious and nervous and tense. And they stopped praying and were worrying about the vandalism that was taking place. And they were losing touch. The monastery abbot asked the monk Andrei Rublev to paint them an icon to help bring them back home, to communion.

"Paint us an icon that brings us back to the place where we belong," he says, because the darkness of the world was breaking their communion. Remember your feelings on the first day of the Gulf War, when you were watching television? How such scenes darken our hearts sometimes. Before we know it, we become an accomplice of the things we are watching. Suddenly we find that our hearts get coarsened. We lose the communion. And we suddenly feel that brokenness inside us. So the abbot says to Rublev, "Paint me an icon." And he paints an icon of the communion of God.

The three angels visited Abraham as a prefiguration of the inner life of God. He painted it in such a way that our own place is right in the front, gazing on this communion. It is where we belong. We are present there and can be lifted up into the communion of the Holy Trinity. This is not simply an illustration of the Holy Trinity or a nice picture to hang on the wall. This is a place to enter into, to sit in front of, to be gradually drawn into, so that from this place you can be sent back into the world and speak about peace and say, "No more. Stop the evil and darkness." From here, from the place of communion, because it is precisely the broken communion that creates the war and the violence that we want to stop.

When Jesus came down from the mountain, he called his

disciples and he formed community. It is really interesting to realize that every time in history that someone really lived in community with God, community happened around him or her. Great people like Teresa of Ávila, Ignatius Loyola, or Dorothy Day, or like other people whom you might personally know, people of prayer, people for whom communion with God was their primary concern, these people built community. Or better, community happened around them.

That is very much the history of my own L'Arche community. Jean Vanier wasn't trying to do something big or organize a big community. He was a man who was very much looking for God. He brought two people around him to live an intimate family life together. Out of that, many things happened far beyond his own expectation or desire.

Communion becomes visible and livable in community. In my own life, I was talking a lot about prayer and about community and about communion, but inside I felt I wasn't living it. Certainly at universities it can be very hard to keep it all together. You give a lecture about community, then you go home and find yourself alone. Or you talk about humility, but then find yourself wondering what everyone thinks about you.

Finding Community

You begin to realize that communion and community belong together. You don't know exactly where and how. When I started to pray more deeply and more intimately, I began to realize I was looking for a home in God. But somehow that home in God had something to do with how I would live with other people. And that's how I finally ended up coming to L'Arche. Community might mean something very different for you than for me: a family, your circle of friends, the people of your parish, or a more formal community like our community, L'Arche Daybreak.

One of the great struggles we have is to live community as an expression of communion. Quite often the way I live community or I live relationship is in a way that makes demands on others. "I want you to help me solve my loneliness," I might say. Or, "I want you to take my anguish away." Or, "I want you to help me overcome this craving in my body and in my soul." I've made many mistakes in my life by going to people and wanting them to offer me communion. I called it "community." But often what I was really asking them to give me was communion, a sense of wholeness, a sense of safety.

And before I knew it, I was harming people. As soon as you ask for communion from another human being, whose ability to love is very limited, you can end up becoming very pushy and manipulative, because you need so much. You go out looking for communion, and you always come home somewhat disappointed.

I see the anguish in so many people who so much want to find this communion, and suddenly they wake up with a deep sadness. It is very serious that every time we go out and want people to give us the communion that only God can give us, there's some sadness. Waves of melancholy come and we feel very deeply that, yes, we were so much hoping to find it, and yet it's not happening. We live our lives with a constant hope: "Let's try it again. Maybe this time." And the world in which we live manipulates our desire for community by constantly suggesting that this or that might finally satisfy the deeper desires of our hearts.

And that's the enormous seduction of the world. "Try this

out, or that, and finally you will find what you're seeking." And so we try it. And our loneliness only deepens. This happens because we want a love that can only be given by the One who created within us that desire for love. Therefore, if I grab on to other people or to situations with that yearning, I constantly find myself doing more harm than healing.

And what I want you to hear is that, first of all, if you come from the place of communion, if you come from the place where you trust that you are unconditionally loved, and if you know that the communion that you most desire is already given to you, then you can enter into community and live with other people in ways in which they can give you love and affection and care that you can receive in gratitude as a sign, as a reflection, of that first love.

One of the things that I experienced when I came to L'Arche was that people who didn't know me, people who have very little ability to express themselves, suddenly made me aware of a love that existed long before any human hand touched me. They brought me in touch with the first love that offers me communion. This is the voice that says: "I have loved you with an everlasting love. I have seen you from all eternity. I have held you in the palm of my hand. You are my son. You are my daughter. You are my Beloved." And what is so amazing is that from the moment that I am in touch with that, I suddenly can enter into community and realize that other people can give me a lot of affirmation. They affirm that first love, even in their own very limited and fragile ways.

I can finally love without wanting the same in return. I can finally give without necessarily wanting to have the same back. I can finally be a little freer among people who I don't find very easy to live with all the time. Somehow I can forgive them for not being God. I can forgive them for not fulfilling all those needs, because I know that what they give me is just a glimpse of that first love. Sure, it is true that I must often live that first love in the darkness, and my prayer at times may feel empty and very dry. But when I walk among the people, I can gradually see that what they give, and what they tell me, and what they do are little glimpses of that love that I know and believe in.

And so community is always a life of gratitude—it's a eucharistic way of living, thanking people for their goodness. You can say: "You're good. Thank you for how you give me a glimpse of that first love. You bring me in touch with that. We need each other." The Christian community is a community in which we keep reminding each other of the first love, while not replacing it. Marriage is precisely a relationship where two people are together and get to point each other constantly to a surrounding love that is greater than either of them alone can hold. That's also what friendship is about. Two people can love each other in deep friendship because they can help each other reaffirm that larger love that cannot be grasped, even though we can trust and believe in it.

I also want to share with you something else about community. On the one hand, it is an expression of communion. But it is also the place where I am thrown back with a spiritual intensity, and forced to encounter the necessity of building a lifelong communion with God. Community is the place where you finally come in touch with your real brokenness. When I share with you about L' Arche, what I have to tell you is that, on the one hand, I found a home there. I found friends. I found people who really love me and whom I can love, and it is beautiful. And at the same time, it can also be awful!

Someone in our community says: "I hate it and I love it."

That's true. And what happens is that precisely when you enter into community, when you enter into friendship, when you enter into a deep intimacy, you always come in touch with your deeper brokenness. You discover your deeper woundedness. Community can expose your deeper pain. I sort of had it a little together until I lived in L'Arche for a while. The people there with their openness and their directness, and being truly loved also touched me in places, but it opened up a deep woundedness that I had hidden from myself in the competitive tussle of academic life. The deeper I entered into the light of community, the more I discovered my own anger, my jealousies, my fear of being rejected.

And there was so much yearning there that I wasn't even aware of. I experienced real friendship and love in community, but life together opened a space where I discovered wounds that I wasn't even daring to face. Community is the place where I can no longer hide out. I can't play games very long with those I live in real community with, or with myself. Community invites us to take off the armor of a successful career. I'm invited to let go of it. And if I don't let go of it, somebody else will just strip it away, anyhow. You are naked, after all. "Oh yeah, you are a priest and you speak nice. And you write these books, but listen, living with you is another thing!"

What I hope you hear is that this is where a whole new call suddenly becomes visible: the call to be patient, to live your anguish, your pain, your darkness with open eyes, and in a way, to embrace it and befriend it as your own. Patience means living the moment to the full, tasting the fullness of who you really are, staying in the place where you are most in pain. Community reveals your pain and then says to you, "Don't run. Don't go all over the world in search of satisfaction, but stick to your place and feel it all the way through. Live it all the way through." If you can live through that enormous desire—even knowing that it cannot be fully satisfied—and trust that it will not destroy you, you will find underneath it something that will finally bring you to new life.

Trust that if you are willing to go all the way and embrace your pain and your woundedness, you will be converted; "metanoia" will take place. To stand in your pain, to touch it with the confidence that if you live it through you will find new life. That's what community is. If you live it through, you will find new life. That's what community calls you to.

It calls you again to communion, to a communion that transcends your pain, but which can only be reached by living your pain, your struggle, your woundedness, and your loneliness to the full. A friend of mine has made it very clear to me in the last few days that if we are not daring to live it through, we end up as moody people. One day, we feel good. Then we feel bad. Like waves back and forth. But living in community calls you to live through all the way to the center of your anguish and your pain, and to hold onto it and to stand there.

Let me say it in a different way.

I was alone and that's why I came to community. But in community, I discovered the second loneliness. As with marriage, or with friendship, suddenly you realize that underneath the superficial loneliness that might be dealt with by having friends and spouses and community, there is a lot of loneliness that cannot be solved. But we have to claim that as a source of energy. It's a very mysterious thing. From the point of our pain we can find new life. There is a loneliness that we should not want to get rid of. There is a second loneliness that you discover in community, that you discover in friendship, that you discover in marriage. You may begin discovering this sometimes when you're forty or fifty. I see a lot of people discovering it with distress and responding to it by saying, "Oh my goodness, my marriage!" Or "My community!" "Oh no, I have to start over."

Could you consider claiming the second loneliness as a place that calls you into an always deeper communion? That way leads you back to the mountaintop to discover communion at a new level, where there is new life for you. Your aloneness lived all the way through may reveal itself as "all-wellness." The nothingness of your life might reveal itself as "no-thing," and as relationship instead. Your experience of "nowhere-ness" might reveal itself as "now-here-ness." It is a way of gradually discovering that precisely in the center of where you are most vulnerable, where you are most in pain, where you are most poor, there God dwells. Blessed are the poor. Blessed are those who mourn. Blessed are those who are weak.

Blessed are you where you are poor. Blessed are you where you are crying. Blessed are you where you are in pain. The community allows you to touch your poverty. It allows you to discover your handicap and allows you to taste more deeply your mourning, your grief. And you are called to believe that it is there where God chooses to dwell. That's what we could call the preferential option for the poverty in you. Jesus didn't say, "Blessed are those who care for the poor." He said, "Blessed are the poor." Not, "Blessed are those who console those who weep," but, "Blessed are those who weep." Community allows you to weep, allows you to feel your poverty, allows you to touch your brokenness. Community stands around you as people who say, "Don't be afraid. Don't run off. Trust that Christ will be born in that place."

That's an enormous act of trust to make that choice. And I

want you to hear that you have the power to choose this way. You can choose to stay in your poverty instead of running away and trying again somewhere else. You can choose to taste your loneliness in a new way and discover that in the midst of your loneliness, there is a blessedness. I've been with people who painfully lost friends or husbands and wives. They stayed away from all social contact for a long time and wanted to taste their loss to the full. They trusted that by feeling the loss completely, a new presence would be made possible.

The disciples of Jesus, after his death, wept for their loss. But they were waiting for the Spirit to come and they prayed together. And if you see them in that room waiting, there's fear, but there's also a holding on to their loss. They tasted their loss together. And as they listened to their loss and their grief, the Consoler, the Counselor, came and revealed God's presence precisely in the place where they were most hurting, most vulnerable. I really hope that you can hear this because it's not easy to say. Precisely where you are most in pain, God touches you most deeply, where you're most vulnerable. There something new can be born, where you're most broken. But only on one condition. And that condition is that you live it as the beloved.

If you lose touch with the truth that you are the beloved, that you are blessed by God, then all these rejections and pains will lead you into darkness and despair. It's only as the beloved that you can embrace your brokenness. It's only as the one who is infinitely blessed by God that you can hold on and say, "I don't want to run away. I want to be faithful to my own pain and claim my pain as my way of being me." Because that's so important. Each one of you, each one who is sitting here is having a pain that you experience as uniquely yours. And it is. You don't have to compare your pain with anybody else's.

Your pain is the worst; that's always true. [Laughter] That's true because it is so intimate. It's so personal. It is your own pain.

You don't have to say, "Compared with what she or he suffers, maybe it's not all that bad." No, no. What you suffer is the place of your pain. And you have to say, it's mine, and claim it and hold on to it and befriend it. Trust that if you let that pain speak to you, its full language, it will finally make you aware that you are even more beloved than you ever realized. That's what Jesus says to the people on the road to Emmaus. "But didn't you know, you foolish man. Didn't you know that the Christ had to suffer? And so enter into his glory." Then suddenly the brokenness becomes the way. And I don't want to romanticize it. I don't want to say pain is good, or pain is just nice. If pain is a call, then hold the call in it to a deeper communion. Yes, you are in communion with this God, but there is a call to go deeper together.

I tell you, the closer you come to communion, the closer you also come to the experience of your own brokenness. The more you stand in front of the Lord who calls you the beloved, the more you realize that you are still holding things back from God, your beloved, whom you don't yet fully trust. "What about this? What about my shame? I'm so ashamed this happened. I'm not going to talk to you about it." But you are the beloved. "Yeah, but only when I am good."

"When I show you the shame, am I still the beloved?" I am still the beloved, when I tell you my brokenness. I'm still the beloved. When I tell you my nighttime dreams that I don't want anybody to know about. I'm still the beloved when my naked truth is there in front of you. God's voice says to you, "Yes, you are my beloved."

That voice speaks to us: You are blessed by me and I will

never take my hand away from your shoulders, and from your heart. I touch you with that love. Show me everything. I'm your Master, I'm your Lord, I'm your Lover. And don't hide anything from me. And you might gradually discover that one source of your suffering that you don't have to suffer is the fact that you are keeping things hidden from God, putting things away in little corners. No. Every time you open one of these little corners, again, the voice becomes clear: "You are my beloved. And you are called up higher to the mountaintop to be in communion with me."

9

A Spirituality of Community

Henri presented this address in March 1992 at a gathering at the University of Notre Dame organized by Rev. Don McNeill, C.S.C, and the Center for Social Concerns. Henri describes our shared humanity as "the fellowship of the weak" and offers it as the most solid foundation on which to build community.

I'd like to share with you about a spirituality of community. And I'd like you to consider three words to remember that I believe are important: *claiming, reclaiming,* and *proclaiming.*

First, we are constantly invited to claim our humanity. And that's not so easy. Certainly not for me. Because the definition of who we are that many of us live with is: "You are the difference you make." That's what my dad said. You are the difference you make. Show me that you are going to be different from other people. Show me what your unique contribution in life is. Show me where you are not like everybody else.

Somewhere that was in me very early on. I was encouraged to compare myself constantly with the people around me, hoping that I would come out a little different, a little better. More handsome or more intelligent (and obviously I didn't succeed at all!).

That's a very basic concern that you have, that we all have, that includes the question we ask of ourselves, "What's the difference that I make?" Quite often we can fall into the trap of thinking: "I am the difference I make." And if that's the main definition I have of myself, then I end up a competitive person. I'm not speaking about competition in that playful way we sometimes experience. But rather in a way that makes our lives about winning in a competition with others. Academic institutions are often very strong on this. Sometimes you discover that you're constantly wondering what other people think about you. You're constantly worrying if you're better or if your grades are better compared with others.

I taught for twenty years at universities. I found that this mode of living made me very strange inside. Because here I was giving lectures about humility and my main question was, "What do people think about me and my lectures? Do they like me or not?" I was giving talks about community life and then when I was home, I was lonely because I didn't want to share all my problems or struggles with others. And I felt, you know, I better be smart here. Here I was talking about vulnerability as a real virtue that God asked me to practice. But I found myself hiding my vulnerable side so I could compete better.

What I would like to say is that there is a whole different definition of who I am. And that is: "I am the sameness I share." I'm not the difference I make, but the sameness I share. Somewhere, I think you as well as I know, there is much more that we share than where we are different. I hope you have some experience of that. Our humanity, our basic identity, is not so much rooted in where I am different. What we share or have in common is so much greater than our differences.

And it's very important that we dare to claim our sameness as the source of our humanity, of our identity. I am like other people and that is worth celebrating. That is what makes life wonderful. Some of you may have heard of Thomas Merton. He wanted to be different until he went into the monastery. And after twenty years of praying, they sent him out for some errand in Louisville, Kentucky. He walked along the street watching people, and suddenly he said, "Wow, I am like everybody else!" After thirty years of praying, I find out I am just like everybody else! But that's so wonderful. Everybody is shining like the sun. All human beings are part of my humanity! And suddenly there was this inner sense of belonging. I belong! I am part of life! I am basically like everybody else.

And that's the source of joy. That is a much deeper experience. It's not that the main mode of my life is competition (in which I try to compare myself with others), but compassion. It means that I am "suffering with." That's what the word means. "*Compatior.*" To suffer with, to be part of. And that is not a reason to be depressed or melancholic or heavy; precisely the opposite.

Every time you really feel part of people in their joy and in their pain, in their brokenness, and in their marginality and in their struggle, there is a source of joy in you that you might never have tapped. This is because the world in which we live is constantly saying, "Be glad because of where you are not like other people." And the gospel is constantly saying, "Be glad where you are like other people, because that's where you are part of a common humanity." That common humanity in its brokenness and its joy is the humanity that God wanted to take on.

That is the main movement of the gospel. It is not upward mobility, but downward mobility. That is, to become like others and discover in your sameness, in your solidarity, in your connectedness and your sense of belonging, to experience there, the joy, peace, the love, the sense of well-being. I think that that's very much what our communities are about. That is not alien to you. That's what family is about. Friendship is about that. That's what life together is about. It's moving from competition to compassion.

I remember very vividly when I was at the university, at a very competitive university in Cambridge, Massachusetts, that constantly was pushing me to be different, how Jean Vanier invited me into community. He did not say, "Well, Henri, we can use you, a priest. We have a lot of work for you at L'Arche. So maybe you can join us." No. He said: "You are always looking for a home (he had obviously read some of my books!), and maybe we can offer you a home. Maybe when you meet core members at L'Arche, like Linda, who always welcomes people warmly and generously with arms wide open, maybe you can find a home there." What happened to me when I arrived for the first time was nobody knew me or what I had been doing all these years. And somehow I sensed I was welcome, really welcomed. Not because I could make a difference. I was welcome because I could be a member of the family.

When I answered that invitation, the community suddenly made me aware that I am not the difference I make, but I am the life I can share. And suddenly I realized that some of the most handicapped people in our community, people who couldn't speak, like Adam, for instance, or people who cannot walk or cannot help themselves, in the beginning, I saw them as different. And they are different than I am. But the longer I lived there, and we lived together, I realized that the difference was really so very little compared with what we have in common. And the fact that Adam cannot speak or that Rosie cannot walk is such a small difference compared with the humanity we share.

I realized that, quite often, those who are most physically in need have the incredible ability to open up in me and others who come from such a competitive society, the place of love. A place where we experience compassion, where we are with others, where we can share life. Obviously that's not just true for our community. This is the gospel story. The gospel story is that the joy, the blessedness, is precisely there where we share our poverty with others.

Jesus didn't say: "Blessed are those who care for the poor." He said, "Blessed are the poor." Blessed are we in our poverty, in our common brokenness, in our common humanity. That's why when you live longer in L'Arche and in communities like it, you suddenly realize that the people who invite you there, the core members who invite and welcome you, are the ones who have a treasure to offer you. You're not there to help them. You are first of all there to receive some of that spiritual joy that comes from acknowledging you are the same. You are not that terribly different.

Linda and I might be different in some superficial ways, but when it comes to our pains and our joys, we really suffer the same. And the longer you're in a community like L'Arche, the more you realize there are sorrows and joys to share, and we're very much the same there. So the first thing is to claim that, our common humanity. Then to realize that these boundaries between those who are capable or not so capable, between those who are old and those who are young, are very superficial compared with the common reality of life. The older I become, the more I realize that I am just like so many other people who in the past I always considered myself to be so different from.

Suddenly I realized that in all the pain that people are living in their intimate lives, their brokenness, their sense of loss, their sense of not belonging, I am not different. And suddenly a love comes from that, a sense of real joy that comes from belonging to the human family. That's the first thing I want to say.

The second is: Once you claim that compassion is our basic call and not competition, how do you live it out? Community life is the place where it happens. Family, friendship, community. That's where the day-to-day reclaiming takes place. You have to keep reclaiming it because you lose it all the time. I lose it all the time. I get jealous, resentful, angry, upset, because I feel rejected. That happens in our community just as much as anywhere else. "Why didn't you ask me for my advice?" "Why didn't you tell me this before?" You know, all the little things.

Community is hard. Community is the place where the person you least want to live with always lives. There's always that one person that you say, "If he or she wasn't here, it would be wonderful." But they are always there. And they dare to remind you of that call to compassion. And what I would like to say is that community is the furnace where our hearts are purified to go deeper and deeper into our common humanity. The invitation, the challenge is to claim that more fully. The two ways in which we reclaim it again and again are forgiveness and celebration. That's how love works itself out in communities.

Forgiveness and celebration. Two words that are very, very important. Because in a very deep way, we want to run away from being the same. We get insecure, we get very anxious. And then we find ourselves trying again to prove that we have worth because we are having success at something. We tell ourselves we are good because people speak well about us. Or we look at our possessions, all our things, and tell ourselves that proves we are wonderful.

If you live in community, you are asked to keep rooting your identity in a very different place. And to do that, you have to keep living a life of forgiveness: To forgive other people for not fulfilling all your needs; forgiving other people for not always giving you that sense of importance that you are looking for. That's a hard struggle because we are such insecure people that we keep wanting to be better than others. We have to keep allowing ourselves to remain anchored in our common humanity. To forgive people their limitations, and to ask people to forgive us ours. Because what you discover when you live in a community is that you are just as handicapped as everybody else. Your handicap might not be as visible, but it is there. In fact, the longer you live in community, the more you discover your own brokenness, and your own limitations. You sometimes have to say, "People, you have to put up with me. I'm going to not change that terribly much. I will try, but I am likely going to be angry again." "And I know you may be the same towards me too. And I have to not try to force you to be different. I have to accept your limitations."

We have to really believe that community is "the fellowship of the weak." It is a fellowship of people who are willing to consistently be vulnerable with one another. And to trust that in constantly forgiving each other for not being stronger or better, and in asking forgiveness for not being that ourselves, something happens that brings forth blessing. The beautiful thing is that when you are able to forgive each other that way, you can celebrate.

Celebration means to lift up the gifts of life. That's what celebration is. Celebration is not simply giving awards to those who are special. That's what the world around us, the larger society, often does. If you are better than others, then you can have a celebration. But to really celebrate in a spiritual sense means to celebrate faithfulness, to celebrate friendship, to celebrate life, to celebrate the pains too. It means to lift up the pains and say, "Yes, it hurts, but we are together." L'Arche is a community with an enormous amount of celebrations. Not parties, but celebrations in which we come together and share what is going on among us. We recognize people and say, for example, "You have lived here this many years now. Let's have a special evening together and talk about your life and share our stories."

Community is a place where we are constantly called to lift up each other's gifts. Not each other's unique talents, but precisely these gifts of friendship, of peace, of joy, of pain, of sorrow that we have experienced together. Sometimes that becomes more visible through involvement with each other. Therefore we keep lifting it up together. The person who suddenly has Alzheimer's. Are we only going to be sad about it, or are we going to say, "How can we care in a special way for each other and celebrate that new call of caring?"

There are times when certain ones of us need more attention, more help than usual. We can recognize and celebrate that together and not just see it as a new burden. This is a constant reclaiming of our shared humanity. The humanity we share becomes more and more visible the longer we are together. It's not true that the longer you are together that it is necessarily easier. Things can become harder, like in a marriage or in a friendship. But it also gets deeper. You suddenly come together at a deeper level.

Finally, I want to say that as a community, we not only want to claim our humanity and reclaim it, but also to proclaim it. That's partly why we're here. I'm happy that I am not alone here, but with fellow members of my community. When I was at the university, I also had to give many talks and make many trips. And people would say, "That's great what you said," responding like it was an individual accomplishment. I'm more and more convinced that as a community of people who share our common humanity, we are called to proclaim that common humanity, wherever we go.

Maybe I could tell you a little story about that.

After I'd been at Daybreak for a year or two, I was invited to give a lecture to a group of priests in Washington, D.C. And these were sort of "higher up" priests at a big hotel in Crystal City, Virginia. There was this hotel ballroom and fountains and statues and all these priests with their black suits and their white collars sitting around tables. And in the weeks beforehand I said, "Can I bring one member of my community with me? His name is Bill." And I said to Bill at Daybreak, "Would you like to go with me to Washington to give this talk to these priests?" Bill said, "Sure, fine. That's great." So he's sitting in the plane and he says, "Henri, are we going to do this together?" And I started to think, "What does that mean?" I said, "Well, yes, sure, Bill."

So people introduced me, and right at the moment I went behind this lectern, Bill got right out of the audience, came up on stage and put himself right here at the podium and microphone, and said, "We are going to do this together." Bill started to turn the pages of my notes. I had it all written out, because I was nervous. And then I thought, "Now I have to say something that really makes people think for a while." So I began speaking, and everyone was listening with great attention, and I don't even know exactly what I said, but there was total silence in the room afterwards. And right then Bill spoke up and said, "Well, I have heard this before."

This was like a little needle in my balloon. But the interesting thing was, from then on, people knew we were together. We were in it together. We were received very warmly. Suddenly all the importance of the occasion changed, and it became people meeting people, and sharing vulnerabilities. Those who at first appeared very formidable and distant, suddenly we all remembered we are just weak people. Bill was the one who could do it. I couldn't do that. Bill in his simplicity was able to reveal to me, first of all, and then to the people there, that we weren't coming up with a big mystery. But we had to proclaim our common humanity. We had to let people experience that in the way we were together.

And so the community of L'Arche is a community that wants to proclaim our common humanity through people who are perhaps marginal, or not immediately central in our society. They offer us an enormous gift to help us reclaim together our common humanity. So I wanted to give you these three words to share what we are about: to claim our shared humanity, to reclaim it in community, and to proclaim our shared humanity wherever we go. Quite often that proclamation can best be done in community with the poor in spirit.

Let us pray. Thank you for just bringing us together, O Lord. Thank you for the fact that we are members of your family, your beloved sons and daughters. Help us to claim that again and again, that we belong to you, as people who are broken, people who are weak, but together we can be strong and proclaim your love. Help us to really live our lives with that kind of awareness that it is good to be together. It is good to belong together. It is good to be human in this day and age. Help us always to say thanks for that. Help us to reach out to each other from that place of sameness, from that place of solidarity. Make us truly compassionate people.

From a Heart of Stone to a Heart of Flesh

Conversion in Community

Henri delivered this previously unpublished presentation on conversion in community life to a retreat gathering of L'Arche assistants in Stratford, Ontario, on December 6, 1995, just over nine months before his death.

I want to speak about the constant need of conversion that we have in life. Conversion from a heart of stone to a heart of flesh. I'm not speaking about a conversion that happens and then it is done, but more about an ongoing desire to let that transformation take place from a heart of stone to a heart of flesh. What would a conversion look like for us? How are we called to that? How are we called to that in our particular L'Arche communities?

I also want to offer a few particular disciplines you might use to keep and continue that process of conversion. What are the disciplines that you need in order to do this? You might say, yes, I'd love to make this conversion, but I don't know how. So you have to know a little bit about the how, and also the what. What do we really want in the first place? If you don't want it, all the stories about how to do it are useless.

The theme of conversion is very central in the whole of biblical thinking. We read about being transformed from the inside, from having a heart of stone to having a heart of flesh. You have that all the way through the Bible. God is saying, "You people have a hardened heart. And I come to give you a new heart. I want you to receive a new heart." So it's important that we look at what this is all about. These are images about how we talk about life and how we have to keep seeking that transformation.

You have to be honest enough to say: "Are there parts of me that are hardened, that are not flexible, that are not moving?" I'm going to describe three ways in which our hearts get hardened. And the first way is by self-rejection.

Self-Rejection and the Hardened Heart

You have to look inside of you and ask yourself, do you love yourself? I tell you there are a lot of people who say of themselves, "I don't really like Henri or Veronica. I wish I were somebody else."

"Now, that *other* person is a wonderful person. I wish that I was like her or like him." And sometimes you realize that, although people like you, you don't like yourself. That's a big problem. A lot of people say, "Oh, Nick is wonderful. Can you imagine being as beautiful as that?" Or "I wish my family were like that." Nick, at his best, might say, "Well, I don't know about that." So the question is, are we claiming ourselves as people that we don't feel good about? That doesn't mean that everything that we are is wonderful and ideal. The point is: Are we happy with who we are? Because the difficulty is quite often, we always say that somebody else is better or that somebody else's life is more interesting. And that your life is just a miserable, insignificant, little life, and you wish you weren't there.

Strangely enough, that is where the hardened heart is often located. You are not satisfied with yourself. "Love your neighbor as yourself." But that is difficult if you don't love yourself, if you're not somewhere well in your own skin, where you can say something like: "Yeah, I'm happy. I'm Henri, I'm tired, and nervous and anxious. I'm always running around. People make all these jokes about me, but that's fine. Deep down, I'm happy that I am me. I can sometimes even enjoy people making fun of me, because I am happy with who I am." But if you don't like yourself, when somebody makes fun of you, or criticizes you, you might say: "Oh my, maybe I am a nobody. Maybe I'm useless, maybe everybody thinks I'm worthless." And so, I tell you something, if you do not feel good about yourself, you will very quickly feel used by others.

So what I want to say is something that might not be immediately clear to you. But if you don't love yourself, if you reject yourself interiorly, and you say, "Oh, yes, everybody thinks good about me, but in fact, I feel awful about me," then very quickly you feel resentful, you begin quite easily thinking that people are using you and mistreating you.

If you don't have a deep self-respect, if you don't have any real sense of who you are, if you don't feel, "I'm well, and I have a contribution to make the world," you can feel like a slave, you feel like somebody who is not very important in other people's eyes, and very quickly, you feel resentful and your heart can grow hard. I want you to realize that this is very concrete stuff, especially when you are living in a community together with others all the time.

In your community you are supposed to help people and care for people and be of service. But if you have an awful feeling about who you are, very quickly, you begin feeling that the people who you help are becoming the ones who use you and manipulate you in all sorts of ways. They are treating you according to your own image of yourself. I was just talking to a nurse from a hospice. And she said, "You know, it's hard for me. Because my patients are constantly complaining and using me, and saying, 'Nurse, go here, Nurse, go there, get me this and get me that,' and 'I need a glass of water.' They are always pushing the button, you know?"

You may feel like a doormat because of how you view yourself. And it sounds strange, but it's really true that if you don't feel strong about your inner life, then very quickly the manipulative behavior around you goes right into that tender place. I'm not saying people don't manipulate you. I'm not saying that people don't use you often, but you feel used and manipulated. When that happens you can become a resentful, angry, and bitter person. You have to see how that works, because otherwise you insist always that other people should shape up, and in a way they have to. But if you don't feel good about yourself, if you don't feel really free, then you become who you think you are. If you think you're a doormat and you are used, then you become it.

Often people say, if you really knew me, you wouldn't like me. If people really knew what I was thinking about, if they really knew what I was feeling, they would think she's an awful person. People think I'm fine. But if you don't love what goes on inside, then you stay in self-rejection. Try to figure out whether that's true for you. That's an aspect of a hardened heart. It spins you right down. Not only in your relationship with yourself, but also your relationships with other people.

Competition and the Hardened Heart

The second thing is that the hardened heart is always competitive. A hardened heart is always trying to compete with other people. Or to say it more simply, "to compare." You are always comparing yourself with other people. You always wonder about the other person. And your identity, your sense of who you are, becomes very dependent on how you compare with others. Am I better? Am I faster? Am I good-looking? Am I smarter?

And competitiveness is an enormous, basic aspect of our society. Look at the papers. What are they writing about? This guy is so fast or this guy is so ugly. Big successes in sport or entertainment, or big crimes. You never read much about a normal life, because it's not interesting.

And so you end up with news that is precisely about where people stick out, where people are different, where people are not like you. We are competing a lot. And children, when they go to school for the first time, they are very sensitive. What do other kids think about them? And if they are liked or not liked—do I have a friend? People are always testing and evaluating themselves. So it's a very basic human quality. If you're insecure, we always want to know how we are comparing with other people.

I am the difference I make. I am by not being like you. And

as soon as you start living competitively, you start wondering about "you and them." Or mine and thine. I tell you that's simple stuff, but it's there all the time. "I have a right to this." "And I want something, because she has something." And very soon you start living competitively in your heart. Very quickly you start interiorly living your life figuring out how much did she get and how much do I get?

How much attention did he receive versus how much did I receive? So "mine and thine" becomes very important. And not just property, but time, attention, and affection. "He gets all the attention." "When I go out with a core member, and everybody is always talking about these core members, they've got such a beautiful personality, but who thinks about me? I'm nobody." They say, "Oh, he or she is so sweet, but they should know how awful that person is who is always bothering me." And I sometimes get angry that, you know, they don't even see me.

And I even compete sometimes with our core members. And there's an anger there. It has something to do with competition, how we feel we are losing in a struggle.

Productivity and the Hardened Heart

And the third question here with our hardened hearts is the question of productivity. We want to be productive people. And you know we want to say, "I produce something, something to hold on to." This is what I got out of my work. And look at it, see the results of it. And by that, I mean, tangible results. The world in which we live is very interested in tangible results. For instance, how much money do you make?

You'll hear, "I work 24 hours a day practically and I get a lower salary than the person who is selling McDonald's hamburgers." "I'm quite willing to spend all my time with handicapped people, but if I had $60,000 a year for it, then at least I'd get something for it. Then I can buy a house, a little scooter and a few things, and then you know, I'll have something. And my life is productive. I'll get some money." Or, "I know a lot of people like doctors and psychiatrists and nurses who make oodles of more money and they work much less. You just have to go to work at nine and get home a little after five. And then you go home and have your family, go out to the movie, or to an opera. They are very popular with other doctors and nurses. And here, we little people, we give our lives the whole day and you don't even get a decent salary for it." So now that's the hardened heart.

Money becomes very important but also other tangibles. You get involved in property or things. Because the relational quality of life does not satisfy. The focus is money, property, and objects. I find it in myself constantly. And when I am no longer satisfied with the relational, then immediately, I'm getting interested in something else to hold onto. I have a father who was very production-oriented his whole life long. So I had these books and the only thing my brother asked me was, "How many copies did they sell?" I said, "Did you read it?" "Oh, no, no. But how much money did they earn?" That's what shows you are important, that you are productive. "My brother wrote thirty books! Everybody buys them!" "Did you read them?" "No, no, I didn't. That's not important."

It's interesting. It's even my nephews and nieces, and they say, "Henri is only wasting his time, working with handicapped people, no one pays much attention to him." But then I was asked last month to be a judge at a big song festival. And they saw me on stage and people gave me flowers, and gifts and bottles of wine, and then suddenly I had "made it" in the eyes of my family, I was a successful person, I was productive. And in the beginning, "Oh, he's just working with handicapped people in some institution in Canada."

So, if you look at these three things—the interior question of self-rejection that makes us feel used; competitiveness that makes us quite often be so concerned about "mine" and "thine"; and productivity that focuses on things and money—then you can see that this whole dynamic is called the institutionalization of life.

The Gospel and Community

But the whole Christian message is to say that we are interested in community instead.

And the core vision on which L'Arche is founded counters and criticizes the way of life of competitiveness and productivity. Competitiveness and productivity are not the basis of life. And if they are, we are part of a world that constantly creates not only tension, but war and conflict. Because if you combine self-rejection, competitiveness, and greed, and compulsive productivity on an international scene, then conflict and wars are the result. Community is saying, first of all, that we are people, children of God, loved by God, and chosen by God. That is at the center of the whole vision for L'Arche communities.

That means that although I might not feel so good about myself all the time, basically I know in a very deep way that I am the beloved daughter and the beloved son of God. I know that I am well in the deepest part of myself. I am a good person because God has created me. So I will live according to that truth.

That's the opposite of self-rejection. And it's very important.

If you have a deep, deep, inner spiritual sense of your own beauty, of your own goodness, of your own belovedness, then you won't feel used. People who are in touch with their own goodness don't feel used. That doesn't mean that sometimes they aren't used. But they don't let that determine their emotions.

They are free. They can say, I won't let myself be used by you, or I have to tell you a few things. Sometimes they use you, then you smile about it. And sometimes you correct people who use you. Or sometimes you say this is not good for you. It's not good for me, but there is freedom in practice and that's very important. And when you're working with people, caring for them or talking with clinical workers, you can say, yes, I see this person is so needy or is misusing this situation.

You can begin seeing the goodness in other people. Then you can start going beyond the idea of "they are patients," "clients," or "numbers that I am hired to help." That's institutional thinking. If you are really in touch with your goodness and your well-being, you have eyes to see that in these people, there is something good. And you call that forth so that their goodness is as real for them as your goodness is real for you. And then the relationships come.

The Gospel, Compassion, and Community

That's first. Then second, we are brothers and sisters of each other. That may sound obvious. But in a very competitive world, that's very un-obvious.

In a competitive world, we focus on the differences, but the gospel is speaking, not about competition, but the opposite, about compassion, "com-passion." "Com" means "with"; "passion" means "suffering." *To be with people who suffer.* Passion means coming through his passion and suffering to be with people who suffer. Competition is the opposite. It is to not be like people who suffer, but to be different from them.

So now what an enormous, important spiritual journey it is when we discover that where our healing begins is where joy is rooted. Not in where you are different from people, but in where you are the same. Normally, I come home and say, "Look, they gave me a prize. I got an A for my course." Wonderful. Why is it wonderful? Because everybody else got a B. If everybody else got an A too, what would be so special about that? That's the spirit of competition.

A lot of our so-called "happiness" comes from that. From rewards, from being a little different. And the gospel is saying, all the great saints are saying, and the whole Christian position is saying, and all that L'Arche is about is saying, is that real joy comes not from being different, but from being the same.

Dean comes and says, I'm from Holland. And I say, Oh, I'm from Holland too. So we start talking and we discover that we have a lot of things in common. And we have a lot of fun and joy in the discoveries.

Imagine the discoveries when we rediscover what we have in common, in our shared humanity and vulnerability: Wow! You are also a human being like me! From the same flesh! You were born just like I was born! You grew up like I grew up. You suffer like I suffer. And you are going to die like I am going to die. That's wonderful! That's exciting!

No, I believe that the real joy is not in being different but in being the same in that sense. That's an enormous spiritual truth. To rejoice in being human. Jesus became human precisely to help us claim our humanity as our greatest gift. Our greatest gift is not that you are black and I am white, or that you are Dutch and you are from the Caribbean, and you are American. That's not what is most exciting. What's exciting is that the differences are only articulations of our shared sameness in a way. There are different ways of being human, we all are human, and if we claim it we can celebrate the differences. What is crucial is that we are all human. And God loves humanity; that is why God became human to include all of humanity in his embrace.

We are brothers and sisters who belong together. Now that's the core vision of L'Arche. We say you are "handicapped," but that's the tiniest difference, whether you can speak or not speak, walk or not walk, compared with the fact that we are both born, we are both poor, we are both weak, and we will both die.

Once I am in touch with that sameness, then I can start to receive the unique gifts that you might have to offer me. Because you know something that I don't know. Or you have a smile that I don't have. Or you can bring people around you in a way that I can't. They are not competitive differences, but they become different colors of the same reality. Now that's what compassion is all about. Compassion means: I want to be with you where you are like me. And that's where healing, that's where comfort, that's where consolation come from.

It's very true, now think about it. I meet a lot of people who have terrible problems that they can hardly do anything about. And you with the core members of your community, they aren't getting any better. They are handicapped and they will always be.

The beauty is we are not called to fix each other and cure each other, but to be together and trust that in being together as brothers and sisters, we heal each other. That is core at L'Arche. There is a healing quality to claiming our sameness. Your handicap brings me in touch with my handicap. I, who feel really well about myself, bring you in touch with your wellness. Even though you might not be able to speak, or you may not be able to walk, or you may not be able to feed yourself. But in a basic sense, you are as loved by God as I am. And I trust that. And you're my brother. You are my sister. You are really me. And so I want to be with you. And I trust that if we are together in suffering, in weakness, in our limitations, healing also will burst forth.

Now our world is not interested in healing at all. Our world is interested in "curing." That is something very different.

A doctor can cure with different pills. You feel better. Sociologists and psychologists have a role. That's good. There's not anything necessarily wrong with that. But the basic call in life is not to cure. Why not? Because you are going to die anyway at some point or another. Curing is not the great event. The great event is caring. Caring is compassion. The same word. Care is the Celtic word for compassion, to "cry out with." Care really is what we are about. Being together in our weakness, trusting that joy, peace, hope, forgiveness, and celebration will come out of that. All the healing gifts that heal us. That's what I see. This is what L'Arche is about.

To bring people together, to live together, to be part of a family, and to rejoice in our humanity together. And we let that rejoicing be seen as a sign of hope in the world. We are not just doing this for each other, but we are doing it for the world.

Shared Humanity, Shared Gifts

I was in Holland just a few weeks ago. I was invited to give a lecture to the European Conference for Mental Retardation. Many people with ties and suits and conference maps. It was like the United Nations, representatives from Austria, France, and many places. I was halfway impressed by it all. You might forget these are all people working with those who have mental handicaps, although there is not a handicapped person in sight. There were screens and movies and lights and speeches. And we discussed in French and German the importance of structural analysis of where we are on this and how we need systemic changes. I just want to give the image of what this was. This was not a community of people. These were people who had a job, who made big salaries, who ran institutions that run quite well, but they had no belief whatsoever that the handicapped people had anything to offer to anybody. They want to normalize them. They have a "right to walk," a "right to have sexual relations." But they weren't discussing ever that people with handicaps had anything to offer to them. And even less that they have something to offer to the larger society.

So what I heard is: "There are people who are handicapped, and that is very sad, and we are a humane society, and therefore as a humane society, we will care for them as well as we can. And maybe it would have been better if they hadn't been born at all. Because then, you know, maybe that's the solution. You know, if people now know that somebody is expecting a handicapped child, you don't have to bring that pregnancy to term. We can prevent this from happening because then we won't need to sustain all these institutions anymore."

And the reason that people start thinking this way is precisely because they don't believe in a deep way that the core members, the handicapped people they're working for, are basically a gift to the world to help us to move away from the kind of life we discussed earlier. They are not really believing that they are our brothers and sisters. That they are just like them; that in the final analysis, handicapped people are brothers and sisters who belong to the same humanity and therefore they have something valuable to offer us.

Fruitfulness through Vulnerability

The third thing is: we are parents. We are not only children of God and brothers and sisters. We are parents. That is, our life is called not to be productive or successful, but to be fruitful.

Fruitfulness is the result of vulnerability. Fruit is born when people are vulnerable to each other. When a man and woman sleep together and have intercourse, they are very vulnerable and naked. They are stripped from power and come together in intimacy, and they can be fruitful. And for a community, if we gather together in a circle and are not trying to play games and we are honest, and we leave behind pretensions, we can be a community, and we can be fruitful.

If you are strong and powerful and keep your distance from others, you might be able to make a product. And many products may create success and wealth. But your life will not become fruitful that way. Your life is fruitful through weakness, through vulnerability.

When people are in Alcoholics Anonymous and twelve-step programs, you come together and say, "I'm an alcoholic or I'm a drug addict and I'm powerless. I need the help of God and your help." And somewhere in confessing this weakness and not having any pretensions, community can be built and we can claim healing power.

It's like the ground outside. If it's frozen, it cannot bear fruit. You have to break it open. That's painful, but then it can bear fruit. Jesus' life is the fruitful life. It's not a successful life. Jesus had no success whatsoever. He ended up on a cross and people laughed at him and despised him. But it was fruitful because somewhere out of a broken heart came blood and water, that is to say, came new life and new hope.

The community of L'Arche wants to be *fruitful*, not very successful. L'Arche needs to be fruitful in order to survive, in order to live. Community has to be fruitful in the sense that we have to continue to come together in vulnerability and trust that as we do that, fruit will grow.

Quite often this may be fruit that you yourself cannot see. At Daybreak I am amazed by that. People come and visit us, and we don't really feel that great about ourselves all the time. But it is amazing how some people say, "I was healed because I came to a place where people are so honest and so willing to share their struggles."

Sue Mosteller and I just finished a course at the Toronto School of Theology yesterday. Thirty-six students from five different colleges. Gord Henry, a core member with Down's syndrome, was part of the teaching staff. In the final class people were crying and saying things like, "This was the most important class we have ever taken." "This was the course that really changed our lives." And I said, "Why?" Because you know, the other professors are just as good as we are. And the main point was "because you guys were so vulnerable." Because you were so willing to share your own struggles. You are so willing to tell us that you didn't have it all together either, but you spoke with hope and conviction in your vulnerability. And somehow you give us permission to be vulnerable too. We could get in touch with our own brokenness and find there the seeds of hope.

That's the difference. You gave us permission to form community in this class itself. There were jokes about this. Because students said, "We have never felt so much community as in this class." And I thought and said: "My goodness, then you haven't had much community, have you?" But still, they were saying that the way they talked and had small groups created space for people to be willing to share their problems.

And why? Because somehow Gordy, Ben, Sue, and I were just together. And we were together in a way that people say, "These people have nothing to hide from each other." And somehow the class suddenly started to say, "Well, why should we hide?" And by hiding, I mean, why should we try to be so strong and successful as students and get our degree and get our doctorates and all this power? Instead of saying finally what matters is that we are people who are fruitful. Jesus says: "Bear fruit." So now these are the three things: we are children of God, brothers and sisters, and parents. Parents in the sense that we bear fruit. You are parents because you bear fruit in each other's lives. We have children, whether they are physical children or biological children, or spiritual children. The priest is supposed to be your father or your mother bearing fruit in the lives of others.

And this is what I call the new heart and the heart of flesh. The heart of flesh is characterized not by self-rejection but by self-acceptance. Not by competition but by compassion. Not by productivity but by fruitfulness. That is what creates community. And you will discover you are always somewhere in between. You're never in a perfect community nor in just an institution. I've seen many communities struggling a lot with that. We want to be community more fully. Are we continuing to practice self-acceptance, compassion, and fruitfulness?

The Disciplines in Community

How do we put into place the disciplines that are required to turn hearts of stone into hearts of flesh, whether for individuals or communities? The core word is attentiveness. Be attentive, be alert, be awake. Be ready. Listen.

The discipline is to be attentive to where conversion is needed. It's not just an outer call; it comes from within. How can we stay in touch with the longing, with the desire for conversion? A lot of people I know have no desire to be converted whatsoever. The fact that you want to be converted is in itself a sign that there is something you long for that you know you are missing. And if you really do live the tension, you are living in a state of longing. If you don't have any tension, if you don't have any longing, you become like many people who finally end up flat and bored. Routine is all there is.

Nothing excites me. Nothing really gives me life. And a lot of people live like that. So be attentive. Attentiveness is the inner goal of conversion. It has to do with attentiveness to the voice of God in your life of prayer.

Prayer and the Longing to Be Loved

Prayer is the place where it becomes possible to get in touch with your belovedness. I don't know if you have ever had the experience of going to a wonderful party and then you come home and feel utterly disappointed. That wasn't as exciting as I thought it would be. It didn't fulfill me.

We often have longings that we project onto a party or a meeting or a person. You come home and you say, there is something more. This person, this movie, this opera, this handicapped person that I was going out with, this meeting at L'Arche—it's all nice, but somehow I want more. I have a heart that desires more. My heart longs for a love that no human being, no party, no core member can give me. And to be in touch with that longing is not easy, because it's painful. Something important is missing that you want. Prayer is precisely to go to the place where you can say, God, I'm not satisfied. I need more love and only you can give that to me.

I need to hear that you are a God who loves me unconditionally, who has molded me in the depths of the world and knitted me together in my mother's womb. You are really my God and the fulfillment of my desire.

Now be careful here. I'm not talking about some wonderful, warm, fuzzy feeling you always feel. Prayer is this statement to yourself and to God that only God can fulfill your needs. Even when that doesn't give you all the feelings you might desire. That's very, very important. You finally have to love yourself and overcome feelings of self-rejection. And you can only love yourself when you know you are loved. Loving yourself means I experience that I'm well held and well embraced, and then I'm okay. I can love myself because I am loved well, and that's a spiritual thing. It's not just an emotional thing. It's not just a mental thing. It's spiritual. Spiritual means that it has an eternal quality that is beyond even the moment of your birth and death.

Prayer and Solitude in Community

First of all, I have a question. Where is the time in your life that you are with God and with God alone? Where is your solitude?

It is really important that there is a moment in your life that you are alone with God. Some days it can be five minutes. It can be ten minutes. But is it anywhere? Is there any place in your busy day that you stop, and you say, "Here I am, this needy, lonely, anguished, confused person in front of you. And I want to hear again that you love me. Otherwise, I may lose it." And if I lose it, then I will go all over the place. "You are my Shepherd. And there's nothing I shall want (though I want all those things!), but you are my Shepherd. So I want to claim that truth. And the truth is that in the deepest sense, all that I need is given to me." That is a real discipline, because everything around you makes you busy, even busy with good things.

Second, I want to ask the question, and it is for your community. Where are you as a community constantly praying to God in such a way that your vision is being nurtured on a daily basis or on a weekly basis? I think you have your regular Monday night meetings, but I just want to raise that question. I have a very strong feeling that if you want to be a vital community you have to have a lot of corporate prayer. I don't mean this or that particular ritual. When do you come together and really hear again that God not only loves you as individuals, but loves you as a community? That you are called together. You don't just happen to be together because you were looking for a job.

That's fine, but that's not the final thing. It's not enough to say, "Well, how are you? Why are you here?" "Well, I didn't know what to do, and I heard about L'Arche." In some cases that may be true, but that's just accidental. That was the occasion for God to call you together. Somewhere as a community, you have to claim your unique, corporate spiritual identity. You have to keep renewing that.

For me that is very, very important. At Daybreak, for instance, we began having a daily Eucharist. Now you may not be able to have that. For us that has become an enormous vital experience. About 40 or 50 people come together each day for just a half hour. And in that half hour somebody speaks, not me, different members of the community, and gives just a little reflection on the gospel.

Together we have an opportunity to say, "I want you to know that I want to live this day faithful to the vision. . . . Now I might not live it perfectly, and I won't, but I want to announce that to you." And so every day there are a few moments when we as a community come together. It doesn't mean everybody. There are 120 members. Everyone shows up some time or another. But most often we are 40 or 50 together.

Basically somewhere it is in the fabric of our life together, that we come together to "re-vision" and to pray to God. Now you might need a whole different shape to that. I'm not at all suggesting any particular shape, but this is something you should think about. How can we keep renewing our corporate sense of being God's beloved body? It is very important. Each of you might have something to say, to contribute, to discern how to live this, no matter whether you have been in this community a long time or not.

Sometimes there are hard things to say when you gather. "It's hard for me to keep loving handicapped people. It's very difficult for me, but I just want to confess that and bring it here." Or you might say, "I just had a meeting yesterday, and something happened that suddenly gives me life." And that's not just good for you, but it's good for others to hear about that. You have to announce to each other on a regular basis, on a weekly or daily basis, the little graces that God brings to you and to share them with each other. That way you can see together that there is something happening here. And we recognize that, and it is beautiful. So, the prayer life on the one hand is solitude, stopping, being alone. On the other hand, to keep coming together as a body to nurture your life together.

You each need to be able to say: "I need to be fed. I need to be nurtured, whether it's by the word or whether it's by the Eucharist, or by somebody who gives a little reflection. I can't live without it." L'Arche is an intentional community and you can only stay a community when you have intentional efforts to pray together. Otherwise it all becomes busyness and work.

Prayer as part of life together is a discipline, an individual discipline and a communal discipline. You as a body are responsible to yourself and to your core members, but also to the future. You may be at L'Arche for two years, five years, six months, but you are part of something, you belong to something that wants to exist for the next generation. I might be dead in ten years, but Daybreak will be there. And I want to do something in Daybreak that allows it to continue. No matter how long you are there, you are part of a movement that wants to move on, part of the visioning, part of the nurturing, part of the spirituality, so that the community feels loved and that those who are there can be loved. So that's the first discipline: attentiveness to God through prayer and solitude in community.

Attentiveness to the Moment

The second is attentiveness to the moment. In the spiritual life there is a very simple statement: God is always here and now. The difficulty is that we are often with our mind in the past, feeling guilty or ashamed about the past. Or we are in the future, worrying about it. We are seldom together, here and now. So the question is, right now, are you here?

To the degree you are here, something can happen. But if you're only thinking, "Now it's 3:00 p.m. and after this I can go there and then tomorrow I can do that," it's fine. But if you are filled with that now, you are not here. You are there. To the degree that you are here, God can do his work. If you would be fully here, this roof would blow up from so much energy in this house. If you and I would be totally here, and nowhere else, this whole building would blow up from the energy. Really, that is what the Holy Spirit is about. But usually you and I are scattered all over the place. To the degree that you are here, God is doing a new thing, he renews your heart, he is reshaping you. So the question is not just "What are we going to do tomorrow?" Or "How I can use this?" The question is: Are we where we are fully, as much as we can be? It's never perfect, it is always limited. And that is one thing that L'Arche is very strong on. The time that is the most important time for community is the meal.

Mealtime in Community

The point is that you say these are moments where we live community with one another around the table. Everybody's there. Perhaps we have a candle or flowers, or a song and a prayer, and we take our time. Whatever you do, we are not eating in order to just fill our bellies and go back to work. We are eating together in community, to be together around the same food and to nurture ourselves. Not just physically, but emotionally and spiritually. So if you don't have these things, I think a good thing for a community to do is to constantly revisit the question: Are we still eating well together? Or have our meals become something similar to fast-food places?

I know a family or a community from the way they behave at the table. It can be: This is peaceful. This is wonderful. I'm welcome here. But if everybody is watching television, others are running off for phone calls, then nobody's really ever there. So to say, we will do everything possible to make sure that everyone is there, that we are not doing other things like telephoning, listening to the radio, or watching television on the side. This is a sacred hour. And in our culture there are very few families who can do that. So it's not obvious in our culture. And I just picked up a McDonald's hamburger yesterday on the way here.

There's the advertising slogan, "You can have it your way." That describes our culture. That's the symbol of our culture. It's not inviting people to create community. So to be attentive to the moment, celebrate the moments at meals together. Also, if you are talking with somebody, be with that person. That's not so easy to be aware that these are sacred moments. The question is never how long. Even when it's five minutes, even when it's half an hour. The question is never how long. The question always is "How full?" If you go to a person in the hospital who is dying, and if you say, "I'm, sorry, I can only stay ten minutes," that's awful. But if you have only ten minutes and you are totally there, that's fine.

Just be there, attentive, for ten minutes. And then if you leave, the person can say, "He visited me. He was really there with me and now he's gone. And he sends his spirit to me. He sent his spirit to me so now he is with me." It's not a question of how long or how many hours. The question is how fully you are there.

In that moment, you communicate that they are the most important person in the world to you. And you are saying: I want you to know that and I want to be here with you. And here, now, God is with you, talking to you. And then when the time is over, I can go. If you are fully present to people in the moment, then you can let go of them too.

That person is fully there. You can commend that person to God, and you can move on and do something else. You may have to go to the supermarket and give your attention to that. You have to pay attention to that. Then you have to be in the chapel and pay attention to that. And then in the house. But you are trying to be where you are and do what you do. The great spirituality of L'Arche is that all that you do is sacred. God can be there when you do the laundry or do the dishes. The difference between a housemate who just does busy work and the handmaid of the Lord is not what you are doing, but the fullness in which you are present to what you are doing.

I go shopping, you go shopping. I do the laundry, you do the laundry. Do we live it as a way to be present to God or as just a chore? That's the difference. "Le quotidien," as the French say. Right there in everyday, ordinary life, in the hidden life of L'Arche, God can be very, very present there. That's the discipline, a real discipline.

Go to the Places of Poverty

The third thing: Always go to the places of poverty. That's a discipline. Go where the poor are. The word "poor" does not always mean economically poor. It doesn't necessarily mean people who sit on the street. But somewhere, go to the places where people are poor, and where you are poor, because that's where you will be blessed. And that's where others are blessed. "Blessed are the poor." So if you want a blessing, go there. Jesus did not say blessed are those who care for the poor. He said, "Blessed are the poor." So, you might be the poor. And your wife or husband might be the poor for that moment. What I'm saying is don't be afraid to go to places where people are hurting. Spiritually, every time you go close to places of woundedness or poverty, you will find light. You'll find hope. You will find joy. You will find peace. You find all the things you ever want. Don't veer away from the places of hurt, but go right there.

I remember talking with people who were quite wealthy. And like everyone else, I'd say, tell me about your job. But people get very bored with this very quickly. But if you say, tell me about your heart. Tell me about what you are living. And this person, who in a way is wealthy and successful in their business, has the opportunity to say, "Well, this is what's been hard for me lately. My colleagues and I are not getting along with each other. Or I sometimes wonder if people really love me. Or I feel disconnected from God or the church." Whatever people say, there are places of poverty and you go there, and you say, "Let's talk about that." You discover that is where friendship is made. Precisely there. You weren't afraid. You listen and you say: "I'm glad to be with you. Thank you for sharing that. I feel closer to you because you shared some of the struggle. And that's a privilege for me." And you hear: "Thank you for being with me."

You come home and say, "Wow, that was a beautiful evening." That person wasn't afraid to tell me something of his or her life. No hiding. Instead of making you sad and depressed, there's a joy that I have had the privilege to enter into the suffering heart of this person, the suffering heart of the world, the suffering heart of God.

But when you forget that, and you begin running after security and wealth, you lose the joy and the peace you are really looking for. But that is a discipline to practice.

It is a discipline because poverty is not attractive all the time. When people are dying, you want to stay away from them. When people are sick, it's hard to knock on the door. Your core members in the community might be going through a lot of pain, and it interrupts your plans. Somehow to really believe that if you keep your focus on the heart, the hidden blessing will be there. It's not wallowing in sorrow. You begin to say: I trust that there's a blessing there for me. A blessing to receive from the poor. And there is a blessing for others to be found in my poverty. That is a discipline that requires vulnerability.

So, the three disciplines: Attentiveness to God where he can say "I love you," both as individuals and as a community.

Attentiveness to the moment, where you can discover God is right there with you in your meals, and in your conversations and community life. And attentiveness to the poor, where God always brings his blessing. That's where the child is born within you. Your heart becomes a place that is prepared to receive that little child. And if you are attentive, you may not even notice it, that God is right there where you are, saying, "I'm here for you. And I made myself very small. So you don't have to be afraid, worried, or anxious."

Sources

The following sources for these chapters have been preserved in the Henri J.M. Nouwen Archives and Research Collection at the John M. Kelly Library at the University of St. Michael's College at the University of Toronto.

Chapter One

Henri presented "From Solitude to Community to Ministry" at the Foundation Conference sponsored by the Buford Foundation in Toronto in September 1993. His conference address was subsequently published in *Leadership Journal* in 1995.

Chapter Two

This reflection by Henri on the role of spiritual formation and community in theological education originally appeared in *Sojourners* in August 1977, in an article titled "What Do You Know by Heart? Learning Spirituality."

Chapter Three

"Finding Solitude in Community" appeared as "Solitude in Community" in the journal *Worship,* volume 52, in January 1978.

Chapter Four

Henri published the article "The Faces of Community" in the March–April 1978 edition of the *Catholic Worker* newspaper.

Chapter Five

Henri delivered the text of this previously unpublished address, "Called from Darkness," in June 1982 to a worship service at Saint Peter's Lutheran Church in New York City to mark the United Nations General Assembly's Second Special Session on Disarmament.

Chapter Six

Henri delivered the text of this address to the Catholic Youth Corps at the University of Toronto's Convocation Hall in April 1987. It is published here for the first time. The Henri J.M. Nouwen Archives and Research Collection maintains an audio file that includes this talk and musical presentations from the event from which this transcript of the address was developed.

Chapter Seven

The article "Holding Ground" is taken from a talk given by Henri Nouwen in March 1987 in Baltimore, Maryland, to Baltimore Clergy and Laity Concerned's March Conference "Responding in Faith as the Americas Meet." The talk was subsequently published in the CALC Report by Baltimore Clergy and Laity Concerned (CALC), Vol. XIII, No. 2, in the spring or summer of 1987, pages 12–20. The original article is abridged here to focus on the theme of community.

Chapter Eight

Henri delivered "From Communion to Community: The Contemplative Journey" at Regis College, University of Toronto, on February 27, 1991. The Henri J.M. Nouwen Archives and Research Collection has preserved an audio recording of this presentation from which this transcript is drawn. It appears here in print for the first time.

Chapter Nine

Henri presented this address on March 10, 1992, at the University of Notre Dame at the invitation of Father Don Mc-Neill, the founder of the Center for Social Concerns. The Henri J.M. Nouwen Archives and Research Collection has preserved a video recording of this presentation from which this previously unpublished lecture is drawn. The presentation was originally titled "God's Love Experienced in Community."

Chapter Ten

Henri delivered "From a Heart of Stone to a Heart of Flesh: Conversion in Community" to a retreat gathering of L'Arche assistants in Stratford, Ontario, on December 6, 1995, just over nine months before his death on September 21, 1996. The Henri J.M. Nouwen Archives and Research Collection has preserved a video recording of this retreat from which the transcript of Henri's presentation is drawn. It is published here for the first time.

Acknowledgments

There are many people who helped bring this book to life. I would like to thank Karen Pascal and the Henri Nouwen Legacy Trust for entrusting me with the privilege of exploring in Henri's archives for these chapters on community. Special thanks goes to Gabrielle Earnshaw who provided initial research of great value. As the founding archivist at the Henri J.M. Nouwen Archives and Research Collection, her labors in preserving and mapping the terrain of Henri's life and work have richly endowed researchers and the worldwide community of those who continue to be inspired by Henri's writing and wisdom.

Robert Ellsberg first had the vision for this volume. Thank you for your editorial recommendations, your keen spiritual sensitivity, and the gift of your foreword, reflecting on your friendship with Henri over many years. Thank you also to Maria Angelini, managing editor at Orbis and her team for the care taken with text and the creativity of the cover design.

Simon Rogers, special collections archivist at the John M. Kelly Library at Saint Michael's College provided expert and timely assistance sourcing manuscripts for review without which the tight deadlines for this project would not have been met during the disruption of the pandemic. Frank Faulk offered helpful comments on an early draft of chapter six. Robert Walker and the Rev. Ajit John planted the seeds of my interest in Christian community during graduate school. Two abiding friends and spiritual companions of many years, Rev. Bill Haley and Rev. Tim Clayton, both deserve thanks for first introducing me to Henri's writings over two decades ago as part of Kairos, a Christian community they led in the Washington, D.C.-area. Your ministry has shaped the future direction of many.

Finally, no words are adequate to express my gratitude to Judith Cooke, my wife, for her support and love during this past year. You continue to teach me much about the power of vulnerability and being available to others in a wholehearted way. Through your counselling practice, your care for our boys, Isaiah and Aaron, and so much more, you labor in love to make a home for God in this world. May this book be a reminder to them and to others that the door to God's house is always open, offering our restless hearts a warm welcome home that satisfies like no other.